# CHILDREN *of* ABRAHAM

*a course in commitment*

**Daniel Gruber**

ISBN 0-9669253-2-7

**Elijah Publishing**
**PO Box 776**
**Hanover, NH 03755**

www.elijahnet.org

# CHILDREN *of* ABRAHAM
## *a course in commitment*

### TABLE OF CONTENTS

| | |
|---|---|
| **INTRODUCTION** | 1 |
| 1. Commitment to GOD | 3 |
| 2. Commitment to YESHUA | 9 |
| 3. Commitment to THE WORD OF GOD | 20 |
| 4. Commitment to PRAYER | 29 |
| 5. Commitment to GROWTH | 41 |
| 6. Commitment to THE COVENANT | 51 |
| 7. Commitment to MAKE TALMIDIM | 60 |
| 8. Commitment to FAMILY | 69 |
| 9. Commitment to PURITY | 82 |
| 10. Commitment to GIVING | 91 |
| 11. Commitment to AUTHORITY | 100 |
| 12. Commitment to RIGHTEOUSNESS | 113 |

# INTRODUCTION

The Bible tells us that Abraham was a friend of God. He lived a life that was pleasing to God. God has made him to be the father of all those who believe, whether they are Jewish or Gentile.

That is why God said, "Listen to me, you who pursue righteousness, who seek the Lord, look to the rock from which you were hewn and the quarry from which you were dug, look to Abraham, your father, and to Sarah, who gave birth to you in pain. When he was one I called him, and I blessed him and multiplied him." (Is. 51:1-2)

When Abraham was a Gentile named Abram, God called him to begin a new people. God changed his name to Abraham, making him the father of the Jewish people. At that time, God also told him that he would become the father of many Gentiles. Through faith in Yeshua, Gentiles become children of Abraham.

Therefore, whether you are Jewish or Gentile, the life of Abraham, your father, is an example to be studied and imitated. Yeshua said, "If you are Abraham's children, do the deeds of Abraham." (Jn.8:39) This is a study of some of the deeds of Abraham, and the character and commitment that they demonstrate. Those who are truly Abraham's children will bear his likeness in their faith and in their works.

In the course of this study, we will use the Hebrew form of names in the Messianic Writings for the people we study, rather than the Greek forms. This may help us to know them as who they were. So, we will speak of "Yeshua" rather than "Jesus," "Miryam" rather than "Mary," "Jacob" rather than "James," "Kefa" rather than "Peter," "Yochanan" rather than "John," "Judah" rather than "Jude," "Shaul" rather than "Paul," etc. Books of the Bible will be referred to in their current, standard English forms.

We will look from different angles at the incidents in the brief record of Abraham's life. It is a life worthy to be emulated.

# 1. Commitment to GOD

The record of Abraham's lifelong walk with God begins with the call to be holy, to belong to and be set apart for God. "Now the Lord said to Abram, 'Go forth from your country, and from your relatives and from your father's house, to the land which I will show you; and I will make you a great nation, and I will bless you, and make your name great; and so you shall be a blessing; and I will bless those who bless you, and the one who curses you I will curse. And in you all the families of the earth shall be blessed.'" (Gen.12:1-3)

A man's country, relatives, and father's house establish most of the structure and content of his life. God makes it clear that we have responsibilities toward all people, and especially towards those in our families. But sometimes those relationships are not kept in their proper perspective, and they hinder a person from wholeheartedly following the Lord.

Rabbi Hertz commented on the way God called Abraham: "These are the main influences which mold a person's thoughts and actions. ... He was to cut himself completely adrift from all associations that could possibly hinder his mission. A similar 'call' comes to Abraham's descendants in every age and clime [i.e., geographical setting], to separate themselves from all associations and influences that are inimical [i.e., hostile] to their Faith and Destiny."[1]

Those who respond to that call are truly Abraham's children. They are identified by more than their physical ancestry. In Isaiah (Is.51:1), the Lord speaks of them as "you who pursue righteousness, who seek the Lord." They are those who, above all else, are committed to following God. Like Abraham, they willingly surrender all that they have, all that they are, and all that they will be. Every other relationship must begin with, and derive its strength from, this primary, greatest commitment of all — our commitment to God.

There were many times when Abraham did not understand why God was doing what He was doing. There were times when he questioned God. Intellectually, it is easy to trust God. If God is, then, by definition, He is to be obeyed. Also by definition, He is good, righteous, and true. The difficulty comes in the anxiety, frustration, and pain of life in a brutal, impersonal world. Does God really know? Does He really care? Will He really act on my behalf? for my family? in these circumstances?

Faith in God, trusting Him, is a war composed of many battles and skirmishes. It is not a creed, it is a commitment. It is a commitment that affects every aspect of life — every thought, word, and deed. What exactly does it mean to be committed to God?

First, it means to accept Him and surrender to Him as He is. That may not be the same as how you think He is or ought to be, or how some religious or academic tradition portrays Him. God is eternally the same. He does not change to fit anyone's preconceptions or conditions. Whether someone accepts and approves of the way that God is, or rejects and disapproves, He remains the same. We are the ones who must change, as He directs us.

Second, there can be nothing that is more important to you than the Lord God Himself. The Lord requires that, "You shall have no other gods before Me." (Ex.20:3)

People can make idols and false gods of almost anything. If you want to walk with God, you cannot insist on having your own way. You must learn His ways.

We cannot say to God, "**IF** You will let me do what I want, associate with whom I want, or think/feel about myself, someone or something else the way I want, then I will be committed to You." Nor can we say, "**IF** Your will is consistent with my mental, spiritual, political, historical, emotional, or doctrinal understanding, then I will do it." God does not conform to our will. We must conform to His will.

God created Adam with a specific plan and order for his life. When Adam rebelled against God, he was asserting his right to forge his own destiny. His rebellion against God was a declaration: "I will be the judge of what I think, do and believe. I will choose the values and set the standards." Adam was denying God's right to hold him accountable. We must not make the same mistake. We must recognize that God has that right.

Third, to be committed to God we must obey Him. The greatest commandment is "Hear O Israel, the Lord our God, the Lord is one. And you shall love the Lord your God with all your heart, with all your soul, with all your might." (Dt.6:4-5; Mt.22:37) Put differently, God requires complete devotion and obedience. After Yeshua said, "This is the great and foremost commandment," he added, "The second is like it, 'You shall love your neighbor as yourself.'" (Mt.22:38-39) It is by loving God with all that we are that we are enabled to truly love our neighbor. This is not easy, but it is what God requires.

## To Know Him is to Love Him

God wants us to know Him so that we can love and

serve Him. Therefore, He has revealed Himself in many ways. To know Him through these ways, you must decide that knowing God is the most important thing in your life, and be willing to humble yourself and obey Him when you know His will.

God told Israel, "You shall search for Me and you shall find Me when you search for Me with all your heart." (Jer.29:13) To know God is to know man's reason for being. It is not something that will help make you a well-rounded person; it is everything. God's will is not one of many opinions from which to choose; it is life.

Yeshua said, "If any man is willing to do His will, he will know of the teaching, whether it is of God, or whether I speak from myself." (Jn.7:17) Whatever we already know to be God's will, we must do. God is very patient and gracious, but we cannot expect Him to continue to reveal Himself and His will to someone who has already chosen to reject it.

These are some of the ways in which God has revealed Himself, so that we can know Him:

1) God has revealed Himself in Creation. "The heavens declare the glory of God, the earth shows forth His handiwork." (Ps.19:1) The more a person sees the order and beauty of all of God's creation, the clearer the existence and character of God become. The Creator existed before and without everything He made. He is more beautiful, and more desirable, than everything He made.

2) God is revealed in man. God made man in His own image and likeness. Although man has corrupted that image and likeness, some of what remains still reveals the nature of God. Sometimes, as we look at man, we can still see a desire for love, for compassion, and for mercy. Sometimes, we can still see a recognition of the difference between wrong and right. In different

ways, the nature of God is still revealed in man.

3) God is revealed in the conscience of man. Everyone makes decisions to lie or to tell the truth, to steal or not to steal, to be unkind or to be kind, etc. We know what we are choosing because God has given us a conscience, a witness in our hearts. We make decisions according to the light that we have. If we reject that light, and silence the voice of conscience, we end up in darkness. If we continually go toward the light, then we eventually come to a meeting with the Lord Himself, because God is light.

4) God is revealed in the Bible. Taken at face value, even if given no more respect than the sports pages of a local newspaper, the Bible reveals God as He is. Some people impose on the Bible ways of interpretation, rationalizations, and their own imagination that prevent them from learning of God. There may be many levels of meaning and application to something in the Bible, but we always begin with what it actually says in the context in which it was said — the same as we do with all other communications.

5) God is revealed through the nation of Israel. He is shown to be the Maker and Keeper of covenants, the Father, Husband, Shepherd, Savior, Friend, King, Warrior, and Judge of His people. All of the historical relationships that God has had with Israel, throughout the Bible, reveal Him to us.

6) The greatest of all revelations of God, the summation of all the others — conscience, creation, man, the Word of God, and Israel — is Yeshua the Messiah. He reveals perfectly, in every aspect, who God is. He is the living Word of God who chose to enter into creation by wrapping himself in flesh, to live as a man among us. He is the King of the Jews. He is the express image of the invisible God. In his life, we see God as He is.

So then, the nature of our commitment to God — whom we come to know through conscience, creation, man, the Bible, Israel, and Yeshua — is total; all that you are, all that you have, all that you hope to be. All your time, all your thoughts, all your words, all your actions are to belong to Him.

1. <u>The Pentateuch and Haftorahs</u>, edited by J.H. Hertz, Soncino Press, London, 1956, P.45

## 2. Commitment to

# YESHUA

God told Abraham, "Take now your son, your only son, whom you love, Isaac, and go to the land of Moriah; and offer him there as a burnt offering on one of the mountains of which I will tell you." (Gen.22:2) The offering of Isaac is the spiritual pinnacle of Abraham's life. It demonstrates that he would not withhold anything from God, the One who gave everything to him. Abraham, the father of the Jewish people and of all who believe, willingly gave his only son, his beloved son, to be put to death in the plan and purpose of God.

God had miraculously enabled Sarah to conceive Isaac, the son He had promised to Abraham. Isaac grew and matured, the joy of his aging parents. Then, when barrenness seemed to be only a distant memory, God, incomprehensibly, told Abraham to offer up Isaac as a sacrifice.

In obedience to God, Abraham took Isaac to Mt. Moriah, bound him, and laid him upon an altar. "And Abraham stretched out his hand, and took the knife to slay his son. But the angel of the Lord called to him from heaven, and said,'Abraham, Abraham!' And he said, 'Here I am.' And he said, 'Do not stretch out your hand against the lad, and do nothing to him; for now I know that you are one who fears God, since you have not withheld your son, your only son, from Me.

"Then Abraham raised his eyes and looked, and behold, behind him a ram caught in the thicket by his horns; and Abraham went and took the ram, and offered him up for a burnt offering in the place of his son. And Abraham called the name of that place 'The Lord will See [or, "Provide"], as it is said to this day, 'In the mount of the Lord it will be seen [or, provided].'" (Gen. 22:10-14)

On the way up Mt. Moriah, Isaac asked his father, "'Behold, the fire and the wood, but where is the lamb for the burnt offering?' And Abraham said, 'God will provide Himself the lamb for the burnt offering, my son.'" (Gen. 22:7b-8) Abraham was trusting God for what He had promised; that Abraham's name, inheritance, and calling would be carried through the decendants of Isaac. He believed that even if he put Isaac to death, God would raise him from the dead to fulfill His promise.

On that day, God provided a ram, not a lamb. But two thousand years later, God provided Yeshua, the Lamb of God. The offering of Isaac — called the *akedah* by the Rabbis — is the visual, prophetic demonstration of what God Himself intended to do. Two thousand years later, on one of the mountains of Moriah, God the Father willingly gave His only Son, whom He loved, to be sacrificed. He did that because, as the sacrificial system which He established at Sinai shows, every individual deserves the punishment of death for his or her sins, but God prescribes a way in which an innocent other can die in our place.

It was by faith that Abraham offered Isaac; and it was by faith that he did not complete the sacrifice. Abraham believed that God Himself would provide the necessary sacrificial lamb. Yeshua, that sacrificial lamb, told the Jewish crowd around Him, "Your father Abraham rejoiced to see my day, and he saw it and was glad." (Jn.8:58) Abraham rejoiced because he saw that Isaac would live and that God would provide the necessary sacrifice.

In ancient times, it was not unusual for a god to require the sacrifice of a son. For example, the army of Israel was defeating the Moabites in battle, and "When the king of Moab saw that the battle was too fierce for him, he took with him 700 men who drew swords, to break through to the king of Edom; but they could not. Then he took his oldest son who was to reign in his place, and offered him as a burnt offering on the wall. And there came great wrath against Israel, and they departed from him and returned to their own land." (2 Kings 3:26,27)

Other gods could be appealed to or pacified by the sacrifice of children; but the God of Abraham made it clear that He would never require or desire that. The prophet Micah asked, "With what shall I come to the Lord and bow myself before the God on high? Shall I come to Him with burnt offerings, with yearling calves? Does the Lord take delight in thousands of rams, in ten thousand rivers of oil? Shall I present my first-born for my rebellious acts, the fruit of my body for the sin of my soul? He has told you, O man, what is good; and what does the Lord require of you but to do justice, to love mercy, and to walk humbly with your God?" (Mic.6:6-8)

The God of Israel does not require that we sacrifice our children. We do not please Him in that way; we do not atone for our sins in that way. God showed Abraham that He did not require it. Instead, God makes that sacrifice Himself, and requires of us that we "do justice, love mercy, and walk humbly with our God."

In humility, we recognize the judgment that our sins deserve, and we recognize God's mercy in placing that judgment upon His only begotten Son. We need the sacrifice of God's Son, the Lamb of God. Yeshua said to those around Him, "Unless you believe that I am he, you will die in your sins." (Jn.8:24) They knew that they would physically die, but Yeshua was saying that without faith in him they would have no atonement. They would stand before God for judgment in the uncleanness of their sins.

The very first man, Adam, chose to be irresponsible and disobedient to God. He chose to disobey God and to indulge the lust of the flesh, the lust of the eyes, and the boastful pride of life. In so doing, he opened the door of his life to the power of sin, sickness, death, and the Adversary. Because we are all descended from Adam, we all receive the ungodly results of his choice — it is part of our human inheritance.

Death is a curse that came upon Adam through his disobedience. God had told Adam from the beginning, "If you do this, you will die." There was no death in the world before that. Death is a judgment of God upon every individual because every individual is separated from Him.

Death is not just a point in time, death is a condition. When Adam disobeyed, he became subject to death. Death, which had had no power over him, now ruled over him and all his descendants.

God is life. Sin separated Adam from God. Death was the natural consequence.

Every descendant of Adam has been born in subjection to death. Every individual is disobedient and a breaker of God's law. Each individual is a sinner by nature and by action. In whatever way, and to whatever extent God's light has been revealed, every individual has, to some extent, rejected it. To reject the light is to choose darkness. The only way to escape the darkness is to say "Yes!" to the light.

Man desires to control his own destiny, life, and death. That is the thrust of his ongoing rebellion against God — "I will be in control!" That was the nature of Adam's rebellion in the Garden of Eden; it was the nature of man's rebellion at the tower of Babel; and it is the nature of man's rebellion today. The serpent tempted Adam and Eve by telling them that they would be as God if they disobeyed God's command. They would no longer need God to tell them what to do. They could establish their own standards, values, and decisions.

The Serpent told Adam that God was lying; that Adam would not die if he rebelled and ate from the tree of the knowledge of good and evil. So Adam ate, and Adam and his descendants became children of death. But there is more to death than just physical death.

Through the prophet Ezekiel, God warned Israel, "The soul that sins, it will die." (Ezek.18:4,20) God is not speaking of physical death here, because that happens to the body of those who are righteous as well as those who sin. It speaks of the death of the soul, a second death. There is a second death awaiting the wicked.

Adam wanted to be wise in his own eyes and didn't want the Serpent to think he was a gullible fool. So he gullibly, foolishly believed the Serpent, rebelled against God, and ate of the Tree of the knowledge of good and evil. Adam chose the knowledge of good and evil so that he could establish his own standards of right and wrong. That brought death into the world. The different forms of sin — pride, lust, rebellion, etc. — are simply the different disguises that death wears before it makes its final conquest.

Our problems today, and man's problems throughout his history, are the direct result of people rejecting the Lord and His standard in order to make their own gods and standards. The only solution is to repent and turn again to the Lord.

Yeshua obeyed the will of God, even though it meant his own physical death on the *tzelav*, and separation from the Father. (*Tzelav* is the Hebrew word for the cross-shaped wood on which Yeshua was put to death.) To the world and to the Serpent, he looked like a fool, but by his obedient choosing to be put to death on the tree of sacrifice, Yeshua overcame Adam's disobedience. Adam's disobedience brought death. Yeshua's obedience brings life to everyone who chooses to believe in him.

Whoever will hear God's truth and accept it, whether or not it is complimentary or convenient, can be set free. "But as many as received him, to them he gave the right to become children of God, to those who believe in his name." (Jn.1:12) In Yeshua, we receive God's nature — His image and His likeness. We are made part of His family.

Yeshua said, "If anyone wishes to come after me, let him deny himself, and take up his *tzelav*, and follow me." (Mt.16:24) The *tzelav* was a cruel Roman form of punishment, designed to maximize shame and pain, unto death. To deny yourself means to choose God above everything else that you might want. He becomes both your motivation and your goal, replacing your desire to be attractive, intelligent, successful, wealthy, popular, humorous, or anything else.

To take up your *tzelav* means to declare that you are dead to this world and its attractions. Others who live for the world and for the things of the world will notice that decision. Choosing to be a friend of God rather than a friend of the world will bring you persecution. "And indeed, all who desire to live godly in Messiah Yeshua will be persecuted." (2 Tim.3:12) We do not seek persecution, but we are told to expect it. By taking up your *tzelav*, you accept the condemnation of the religious and political leaders of this world. You declare that you are willing to be persecuted, condemned, and killed for following Yeshua.

To some extent, all of us want people to think and speak well of us. Yeshua told his followers to so live their lives that men would glorify their Father in heaven. (Mt.5:16) Receiving the praise of men is not necessarily a bad thing, but it is not something that we should seek. We must choose God's way and His praise, no matter what men may think. We prefer the approval of God and the condemnation of the world to the approval of the world and the condemnation of God. At the most basic level, since this world is at war with God, we cannot be approved by both. "Whoever wishes to be a friend of the world makes himself an enemy of God." (Jacob 4:4)

To follow Yeshua means to desire to live as he lived, even if it means paying the price that he paid. You want to know him, be like him, and do his will. The God of Israel, the God of Abraham, is "Holy, Holy, Holy," making clear distinctions between right and wrong, clean and unclean, good and evil, darkness and light. Whether we understand or like those distinctions, we accept them and live accordingly in choosing Him above and beyond all of man's reasonings and understanding.

For those who receive Yeshua, his death on the tree frees us from the final consequences of Adam's rebellion, and gives us a new inheritance. We are reinstated, with the image of God forming anew within us. When we see Him face to face, that image will be completely formed. (1 Yochanan 3:3) We are not subject to the second death. Without Yeshua, all the children of Adam are totally, absolutely, lost and guilty before God, without any hope of escape, reprieve, or pardon.

Some people say, "Well, WE don't need Yeshua, because WE can go directly to God ourselves." Unfortunately, that is not what the Bible and the history of Israel teach. At Sinai, Israel said to Moses, "Speak with us yourself and we will listen; but do not let God speak with us, lest we die." (Ex.20:19) They asked for an intermediary, someone to stand between them and a Holy God. They knew that they could not, in their sins, come before God Almighty and live. Moses was the mediator of the covenant made at Sinai.

In the covenant of the Law, God instituted a priesthood that mediated direct contact with Him. Only these priests, the *kohanim*, could enter the Holy Place — only in the requirements of their service. No one, except the High Priest, the Kohen HaGadol, could enter the Holy of Holies, where the visible presence of God (the Shekhinah) dwelt. He could only enter it once a year, on Yom Kippur. If even the Kohen HaGadol were to have entered at any other time, God would have put him to death.

On Yom Kippur, the Kohen HaGadol came with the blood of atonement for his own sins and the sins of his family, and then with the blood of atonement for the sins of Israel. No one else was ever allowed to go directly into the presence of God. Central to the Law is the requirement of a covenant Mediator, a Kohen HaGadol, and the blood that makes atonement for sin.

Moses prophesied, "The Lord your God will raise up for you a prophet like me from among you, from your brothers — you must listen to him. This is according to all that you asked of the Lord your God in Horeb on the day of the assembly, saying, 'Let me not hear again the voice of the Lord my God, let me not see this great fire anymore, lest I die.'"(Dt. 18:15-16) Rabbi

Hertz comments, "Israel had refused the high honor of hearing directly the voice of God. As Moses was the intermediary at Horeb, so the prophets shall be the intermediaries in their generation." [1]

There is a sense in which the prophets were intermediaries in speaking for God as Moses did, because the people did not want to hear directly from God. Moses, however, was referring specifically to a particular prophet like unto himself in stature, and even greater.

For the Lord said to Moses, "I will raise up a prophet from among their countrymen like you, and I will put My words in his mouth, and he shall speak to them all that I command him. And it shall come about that whoever will not listen to My words which he shall speak in My name, I Myself will require it of him." (Dt.18:18-19) All of Israel would be required to obey this particular prophet.

As we are reminded in the last verses of Torah: "And there has not arisen a prophet since in Israel like unto Moses, whom the Lord knew face to face; in all the signs and the wonders, which the Lord sent him to do in the land of Egypt, to Pharaoh, and to all his servants, and to all his land; and in all the mighty hand, and in all the great terror, which Moses did in the sight of all Israel." Dt. 34:10-12

The particular prophet the Lord promised is Messiah. The prophecy says that he will do great signs and wonders as Moses did. Like Moses, he will redeem Israel from slavery, and bring God's Law to the people.

The entire system of the Covenant of the Law proclaimed the need for an intermediary — Moses, the kohanim, the Kohen HaGadol, the sacrifices, and the prophets — someone to speak for God to the people and to plead for the people before God. In promising to raise up a prophet equal to Moses, God was proclaiming that even in the future, Israel would need an intermediary.

The Rabbis speak of *Zacuth Aboth*, the merits of the Fathers, as being intermediate between Israel and the judgment of God. God is asked to forgive Israel because of the merits of the Fathers. The Messianic Writings say that God loves Israel because of the Fathers (Rom.11:28), but that the merits of the Fathers are not sufficient for the salvation of their children. Israel is beloved of God for the sake of the Fathers, but not forgiven for their sake.

Even our Fathers had sins of their own. Consider the fact that Abraham lied about Sarah (Gen.12:10-20); and pleaded with God that Ishmael, the son of Sarah's servant, would be his heir even though God had promised him a son through Sarah. (Gen.17:15-21) Or consider that God had chosen Isaac's son Jacob, but Isaac loved his other son Esau because of the wild game he brought him (Gen.25:20-28). Isaac also lied about Rebekah. (Gen.26:7-11) Jacob deceived his father Isaac.

Moses also had his own problems. So did Aaron. Because of their disobedience, God would not let either of them enter the promised land. These all were men of God, but they had human shortcomings and sins. It would be a tragic mistake to trust in their merits as grounds for entering the kingdom of God.

Yeshua the Messiah is the only one ever descended from Adam with no sins of his own. He offered his own blood for the atonement of the sins of Israel and all the world. He brings us a New Covenant that is written directly upon our hearts. His atoning death tore open the veil into the Holy of Holies, giving us direct access into the very presence of God. "For there is one God, and one mediator between God and man, the man

Yeshua the Messiah." (1Ti.2:5)

The natural condition of the children of Adam is one of being lost, hopeless, condemned to death, and guilty before God for eternity. But God promised Abraham a future descendant who would bring blessing to all the earth. (Gen.22:18) "God did not send the Son into the world to condemn the world, but so that the world might be saved through him." (Jn.3:17) Men are already condemned, because "the light has come into the world, and men loved the darkness rather than the light because their deeds were evil." (Jn.3:19) Without a total commitment to Yeshua, men will stand before the Judge of all the earth without an advocate, without God and without hope. Most people will be in that situation.

They do not want a holy, humble, suffering, obedient savior. Instead, they want an anti-Messiah, someone who is the opposite of Yeshua.

They are looking for an Adam who gets away with rebellion against God; someone who has the wisdom of man instead of the wisdom of God, the righteousness of man instead of the righteousness of God, the power of man, etc. One day they will get what they want — the Adversary of Messiah, the opposite of what Messiah is. He will come, and people will invite him to rule over them.

They do not understand the condition of man. They have denied it, and chosen to believe what is not true instead. To know the truth is to know your need for a savior. Yeshua is the only savior there is. Humble, patient, kind, gentle, truthful, faithful, holy and obedient. He is God's love to us.

1. <u>The Pentateuch and Haftorahs</u>, edited by J.H. Hertz, Soncino Press, London, 1956, P.827

# 3. Commitment to

# THE WORD OF GOD

Abraham knew what God wanted of him because God spoke directly to him. And although Abraham did not have the whole Bible to reveal God's will to him, he was in possession of, in either oral or written form, the history of God's dealings with man from the beginning. However much of the Word of God he had or heard, Abraham obeyed it and communicated it to others. His children have that same commitment to obey and communicate it.

There is a rabbinic tradition that Abraham studied in the tents of Shem, the son of Noach, to learn how to worship God. There was plenty of time for him to do that, because Shem did not die until Abraham was 150. Isaac was then 50, ten years before Jacob was born. Shem was 385 when his great, great, great, great, great, great, great grandson Abraham was born, and 460 when God called Abraham to Himself to create a new people.

The last person that God had called in such a special way was Shem's father Noakh. Abraham would have wanted to learn all that he could from Shem, who was the oldest living man, the only one alive who had lived before the flood. Likewise, Shem must have been very interested in teaching Abraham, God's chosen one, everything that he could about the past and about serving God.

Shem had witnessed the rebellion of Nimrod and the building of the Tower of Babel. He had seen his own descendants, and those of his brothers, become scattered into the different nations (goyim) of the earth. Shem had helped build the ark, store the necessary provisions, and gather the animals. He — along with his wife, his two brothers and their wives, and his father and mother — had been inside the ark when God caused it to rain 40 days and 40 nights to blot out "all existence that was upon the face of the land, from man to animals to creeping things and to birds of the heavens." (Gen. 7:23) Shem had seen the first rainbow, the covenant sign after the flood.

Before the flood, Shem had known Methushelach, who lived on the earth longer than any other human being. Methushelach had known Adam, the very first man. Shem was 100 when Methushelach died. Methushelach knew that God had told Noach to begin building the ark because the Lord had said, "The end of all flesh has come before Me; for the earth is filled with violence because of them; and behold, I am about to destroy them with the earth."(Gen.7:13)

Methushelach knew that there was a direct relationship between the completion of the ark, the flood of judgment to come, and his own death. The name Methushelakh means, "when he dies, it will be sent." His name was a prophetic sign of judgment to come. Methushelakh must have watched the building of the ark with intense interest. The sons of Noakh, as they grew up and participated in the building of the ark, must likewise have been intensely interested in all that they could learn from their great grandfather, who had known Adam himself.

Adam lived 930 years. When he was 687, Methushelakh was born. Every time he saw Methushelakh or heard his name, Adam must have been continually reminded of his own rebellion in the Garden of Eden and its consequences. Methushelakh must have wanted to hear again and again the account of man's beginning and sin — the cause for the judgment that would follow his own death.

From Adam to Methushelakh to Shem to Abraham, the necessary details of man's history and relationship with God were transmitted orally and possibly also in writing. Each successive generation, or the divinely chosen individual in that generation, was responsible for preserving and communicating the history of what had gone before.

## The Written Word

The Bible is a book of history, but it is also much more than that. Some people study the Bible as a work of literature. Great literature contains many truths of life in various forms. The Bible contains ALL the essential truths of life presented through history, drama, tragedy, poetry, oratory, etc. As almost all literature and people do, it speaks sometimes with metaphors, parables, and literary devices. When taken at face value within its context, it is usually easy to understand in its plain sense.

The word Bible means "book." It is one book, with many facets, many lessons. As those facets are understood and those lessons are learned, the Bible emerges as THE BOOK to live by. It is the standard by which all else can, should, and must be judged. Some of the facets and corresponding lessons concern the recording of: 1) History, 2) Covenants, 3) Guidelines for Life, 4) God's Power and Intervention, and 5) Memorials and Judgments.

**1) History:** In Genesis 5, we are told that, "This is the book of the generations of Adam." The Bible records particular events that happened to particular people at particular times. By recording historical events, it shows man his own nature — both as he was created and as he is in rebellion — and it shows him the nature of God. It demonstrates what is pleasing to God and what brings His judgment, i.e. it shows all people how to live.

"Now these things happened to them as an example, and they were written for our instruction, upon whom the ends of the ages have come." (1 Cor.10:11) The Bible gives us history — the experience of others — so that we can have roots in the past, and so that we can apply its timeless lessons to our own lives.

**2) Covenants:** The Bible contains many covenants, which are like contracts — i.e., legal relationships. Some of these covenants are between God and individuals; and some are between God and His people Israel. God communicated His Covenant of the Law with Israel to Moses at Mt. Sinai. "Then he (Moses) took the Book of the Covenant and read it in the hearing of the people, and they said, 'All that the Lord has spoken we will do, and we will be obedient.' So Moses took the blood of the sacrifice, sprinkled it on the people and said, "Behold the blood of the Covenant which the Lord has made with you in accordance with all these words." Ex.24:7,8) In a covenant, God establishes specific terms and consequences for obedience and disobedience. The covenant is ratified and sealed in the blood of the sacrifice.

Because of Israel's continual turning away from the Lord, God promised a new covenant, a new agreement, to enable Israel to live and not die. " 'Behold, the days come,' says the Lord, 'that I will make a new covenant with the house of Israel, and with the house of Judah; not like the covenant that I made with their fathers when I took them by the hand to bring them out of Egypt, which they broke, although I was a husband to them.

But this will be the covenant that I will make with the house of Israel; After those days,' says the Lord, 'I will put My law in their hearts, and will be their God, and they shall be My people. And they shall teach no more every man his neighbor, and every man his brother, saying, Know the Lord, for they shall all know Me, from the least of them unto the greatest of them,' says the Lord, 'for I will forgive their iniquity, and I will remember their sin no more.'"(Jer.31:31-34)

"A new heart I will also give you, and a new spirit I will put within you: and I will take away the stony heart out of your flesh, and I will give you a heart of flesh. And I will put My Spirit within you, and cause you to walk in My statutes, and you shall keep My judgments, and do them."(Ezek.36:26-27)

This specific promise of a New Covenant — a new, vital, and living relationship with God — emphasizes God's desire to provide reconciliation and restoration. God offers a covenant that brings the forgiveness of sins, the desire to walk in His ways, and the power of the Ruakh HaKodesh to fulfill that desire. God writes the New Covenant on our hearts so that it won't depart from us, and so that we won't depart from it. Yeshua brought the New Covenant in power and holiness, ratified and sealed in his blood.

**3) Guidelines for Life:** The Bible is life's manual for every individual, society, and government. God is called, rabbinically, "the Governor of the universe." He is THE Governor who has established different kinds of government — self, family, congregational, civil, etc. — which are all to function according to the guidance, restrictions, and regulations laid out in the Bible.

The Bible presents the guidelines by which everyone, whether king or servant, man or woman, parent or child should live. Because the king was to lead and be an example for the people, he was commanded to write out the entire covenant for himself to insure that he knew its contents — his commitment, his responsibility, and his accountability. That would probably be profitable for anyone. He was commanded to read and obey it all the days of his life.

The person who is committed to God's Word will live successfully. Even as God told Yehoshua, "Be careful to observe all the Law which Moses, My servant, commanded you; do not turn from it to the right or to the left so that you may have success, prosper, act wisely wherever you go. This Book of the Law shall not depart from your mouth but you shall meditate on it day and night so that you may be careful to do according to all that is written in it; then you will make your way prosperous and then you will have success." (Josh.1:6-8)

**4) God's Power and Intervention:** The Bible is a supernatural book, given by God, recording and promising His miraculous power. The lesson of the Exodus, and of all redemption, is that God intervenes supernaturally in the affairs of men. The lesson of the conquest of the land of Israel (when the sun and the moon obeyed Yehoshua's command to stand still) is that God goes forth supernaturally with His people. The lesson of the Book of Judges is that God rules in the affairs of men. And on and on through every book of the Bible. The Bible is a book of the miraculous, because God is a God of the miraculous. To eliminate the supernatural is to eliminate God.

Daniel knew that Israel had been in captivity in Babylon for seventy years, the length of captivity that Jeremiah had prophesied. So Daniel prayed and fasted, confessing the sins of Israel, seeking the Lord for fulfillment of His promise. God's Word gave him both understanding and faith. Despite "geopolitical reality," he trusted God's Word as the eternal, unchanging Truth. And as God had promised, He prepared a way for Israel to return from captivity.

**5) Memorials and Judgments:** In the Covenant of the Law, God commanded the keeping of Passover, the wearing of His Word between the eyes, the blowing of trumpets, etc. as memorials. In the New Covenant, we are commanded to partake of matzah and the cup of redemption as a memorial of the Lord's death. A memorial is a symbol that reminds us of something great that was done. War memorials remind us of the great sacrifices that have been offered to preserve our freedom. Memorials serve to remind us to be grateful.

Sometimes memorials remind us to be vigilant in the present, and to be prepared for the future. Even after the supernatural restoration from Babylonian captivity, most of the returned remnant turned away from the word of the Lord. "Then those who feared the Lord spoke to one another and the Lord gave attention and heard, and the Book of Remembrance was written before Him for those who fear the Lord and who esteem His name. 'And they will be mine,' says the Lord of hosts, 'on the day that I prepare my own possession, and I will spare them. I will have compassion on them as a man has compassion on his own son who serves him. So you can again distinguish between the righteous and the wicked, between one who serves God and one who does not serve Him.'" (Mal.3:16-18)

God sees those who fear His Name. When He comes to settle accounts, they will belong to Him. They are righteous, because they serve Him. God also sees those who neither fear nor serve Him. When He comes, they will receive their just reward as well.

# The Spoken Word

The Word of God also comes to us, as it did to Abraham, in oral form. God speaks to people. He speaks to everyone, but most are not listening. Before Israel entered the Promised Land, Moses reminded them, "And He humbled you and let you be hungry, and fed you with manna which you did not know, nor did your fathers know, that He might make you know that man does not live by bread alone, but man lives by every word that proceeds out of the mouth of the Lord." (Dt.8:3)

When the Accuser was testing Yeshua in the wilderness, Yeshua responded, "It is written, 'Man shall not live on bread alone, but on every word that proceeds out of the mouth of God.'" (Mt.4:4) When Eliyahu stood before the Lord, God sent a great strong wind, and an earthquake, and a fire, but He was not in any of these mighty things. Then Eliyahu heard a gentle blowing, a still small voice; and the Lord spoke to him in that way.

There is a human tendency towards routine. A book with fixed rules is easier to follow than a God who makes every day new, and requires that we keep our eyes on Him. The Lord warned Jeremiah of coming judgment and told him why it was coming: "For my people have committed two evils: They have forsaken Me, the fountain of living waters, to hew for themselves cisterns, broken cisterns, that can hold no water." (Jer.2:13) God is a fountain of living waters, but man tries to contain Him in broken cisterns — containers crafted by man out of earthly materials.

God wants us to be in a living relationship, dependent upon Him. Man naturally prefers to have everything laid out in advance so that he won't have to be dependent upon God. But, God's Word and Life itself flow out of Him. Like the manna, it must be gathered fresh every day. God wants us to draw near to Him, not just obey the rules. That is why the Lord says, "I will instruct you and teach you in the way which you should go; I will counsel you with My eye upon you. Do not be as the horse or as the mule which have no understanding, whose trappings include bit and bridle to hold them in check, otherwise they will not come near to you." (Ps.32:8-9)

With God Himself as the desire of our hearts, we look to Him continually. Even an All-Star athlete needs to be constantly aware of the signals that his coach is sending. The coach sees a bigger picture. We are to be so ever-attentive to God that we know the movement of His eye upon us. We are to be so conscious of Him that even His silent glance can direct our lives.

## The Living Word

Yeshua is the Word of God made flesh. He is God's message to the world. His life — including his death and resurrection — is both THE example for us, and the message that we communicate to others. As we deny ourselves and say "Yes" to him, his life flows through us. From the inside out we are changed and become more like him. And when he appears, "we shall be like him, because we shall see him just as he is. And every one who has this hope fixed on him purifies himself, just as he is pure." (1 Jn.3:2)

The written Word of God provides the framework for our lives. The spoken Word of God gives us specific direction within that framework. The living Word of God is the perfect example of how we should live before God and before the world.

# 4. Commitment to

# PRAYER

Prayer is communication with God — talking to Him, and hearing from Him. In this respect, the whole record of Abraham's life is interwoven with prayer. The first time that Abraham's words to God are recorded for us is in Genesis 15.

"After these things the word of the Lord came to Abram in a vision, saying, 'Do not fear, Abram, I am a shield to you; your very great reward.' And Abram said, 'O Lord God, what will You give me, since I am childless, and the heir of my house is Eliezer of Damascus?' And Abram said, 'Since You have given no offspring to me, one born in my house is my heir.'" (Gen.15:1-3)

The first concern that Abraham expressed to the Lord was for his family, which God had promised would be a blessing to all the nations of the earth. How could his family be that, how could he pass on to them what he had received, if he had no son? Abraham had great possessions and great promises from God, but he was not content with material or spiritual wealth for himself.

Because of the cry of Abraham's heart, expressed in prayer, for a family he did not see or know, God could reveal things to him. Before God destroyed Sedom and Amorrah, He told Abraham what He was about to do. These were cities so wicked that their stench ascended to heaven. To cleanse the earth, God had determined to destroy them completely.

Yet Abraham began to intercede with God on their

behalf, as God knew he would. Why would anyone intercede for Sedom and Amorrah? Why would anyone care? The more understandable response would have been, "Thank you Lord! It's about time You judged them for their sins!"

"And Abraham came near and said, 'Will you indeed sweep away the righteous with the wicked? Suppose there are fifty righteous within the city; will You indeed sweep it away and not spare the place for the sake of the fifty righteous who are in it? Far be it from You to do such a thing, to slay the righteous with the wicked, so that the righteous and the wicked are treated alike. Far be it from You! Shall not the Judge of all the earth do justice?'"(Gen.18:23-25)

On the basis of God's justice, Abraham was saying, "Don't let the judgment which the wicked deserve fall upon the righteous. That would be unrighteous." On the basis of God's mercy, Abraham was saying, "Spare all the inhabitants of the city, including the wicked, for the sake of the righteous." God was willing to do what Abraham asked of Him; to spare the whole city even if there were only ten righteous men in it. In fact, in telling Abraham of the imminent destruction, God was giving him the opportunity to intercede. "'As I live!' declares the Lord God, 'I take no pleasure in the death of the wicked, but rather that the wicked turn from his way and live. Turn back, turn back from your evil ways!'" (Ezek.33:11)

"Now Abraham arose early in the morning and went to the place where he had stood before the Lord." (Gen.19:27) Abraham got up early to see what had happened. Had God found ten? "And he looked down over Sedom and Amorrah and he saw the smoke of the land ascended like the smoke of a furnace." (Gen.19:28)

Abraham, like God, had compassion. So he prayed,

trusting in God, and in His justice and His mercy. In this case, there was no remedy for the inhabitants of Sedom and Amorrah, so judgment fell. However, Abraham demonstrated what was in his heart, and what should be in ours as well.

Love for God brings forth love for people. "If someone says, 'I love God,' and hates his brother, he is a liar; for the one who does not love his brother whom he has seen, cannot love God whom he has not seen." (1Jn.4:20) Love for God produces prayer, communication with Him. Love for other people produces prayer — the fervent desire for God's will to be done in their lives. Because Abraham loved people and loved God, he prayed.

Yeshua prayed because he loved people and because he loved his Father. An ongoing relationship with God means ongoing prayer. In a relationship where communication is possible, communication is necessary. The purpose of prayer is not so much to get things from God, but to get close to God. If we belong to Him, then we long to talk to Him, hear from Him, and be with Him.

"He who dwells in the shelter of the Most High will abide in the shadow of the Almighty." (Ps.91:1) If you live with God, He will protect and go before you. "You will make known to me the path of life; in Your presence is fulness of joy; in Your right hand there are pleasures forevermore." (Ps.16:11) If you dwell in the presence of the Lord, you will have joy and eternal pleasures, and you will know the way to life. "And this is eternal life, that they may know You, the only true God, and Yeshua the Messiah, whom You have sent." (Jn.17:3)

The greatest purpose of prayer is to know God and to be known by Him. Your most intimate relationship should be with Him. He promises to guide us as we walk before Him. (cf. Ps.32:8-10)

God wants us to know Him so well that even the slightest movement of His eye upon us is sufficient to direct us in the way we should go. God is almighty — there is nothing that needs to be done that He cannot do — but much that He wants done remains undone because His people do not live a life of prayer.

The Lord spoke to Jeremiah about false prophets and the coming judgment on Yerushalayim: "But who has stood in the council of the Lord, that he should see and hear His word? Who has given heed to His word and listened?... I did not send these prophets, but they ran. I did not speak to them, but they prophesied. But if they had stood in My council, then they would have announced My words to My people, and would have turned them back from their evil way and from the evil of their deeds." (Jer. 23:18,21-22)

The judgment that came on Yerushalayim, and the consequent Babylonian exile, could have been averted if the false prophets, instead of encouraging the people in their rebellious ways, had prayed continually, heard from the Lord, and delivered His message to the people. God desires to forgive rather than to judge, but there must be people who stand in His council and intercede.

All the power of God can be unleashed through our prayers, but we must be living obediently. Shaul encouraged Timothy, "First of all, then, I urge that entreaties and prayers, petitions and thanksgivings, be made on behalf of all men, for kings and all who are in authority, in order that we may lead a tranquil and quiet life in all godliness and dignity. This is good and acceptable in the sight of God our Savior, who desires all men to be saved and to come to the knowledge of the truth." (1 Tim.2:1-4)

In praying, we recognize God for who He is. When

we pray aright, we humble ourselves, because we recognize that we are asking God to do what we cannot do. We demonstrate a dependence upon Him and a faith in Him. In praying and yielding our lives to God, we enable Him to guide, empower, and use us to accomplish His desires in the earth.

God has work for you to do, but His purpose for your life is greater than that work. He wants you to have a vital relationship with your heavenly Father. Yeshua despised the shame of public crucifixion so that he might bring many sons unto glory. He wanted you to be able to come into the presence of the Father.

Even if you do your work better than anyone else in the world, you may still be missing a major purpose of the work. "Whatever you do, do your work heartily, unto the LORD and not unto man." (Col.3:23) To do your work unto the Lord, you must pray. What you do may be good; it may help people or even bring them into the kingdom of God; but what is essential for you is that you grow in your relationship with your heavenly Father.

There are many things that can be accomplished through prayer, many needs which can be met. Through prayer we receive strength to overcome temptation. Sometimes temptation can be overcome by simple will power, but if you trust in your own strength, someday you will fail. If you trust in the Lord, and develop the habit of relying on His strength, you will overcome. God is able to make you stand, and the victory is for His honor and glory.

When we humble ourselves to pray, we are in a position to exalt God. "God is opposed to the proud, but gives grace to the humble." (Jacob 4:6) When we humble ourselves, it is easy for us and for others to acknowledge how great God is.

When we pray and humble ourselves before the Lord, we can receive His wisdom. God knows everything, and wants us to know everything that we need to know. "If any of you lacks wisdom, let him ask of God, who gives to all men generously and without reproach, and it will be given to him."(Jacob 1:5)

As we yield ourselves in prayer to the Lord, the love of God fills us, enabling us to love our neighbor. How can you love your neighbor without praying? If you love someone, you want what is best for that person, and so you pray accordingly. Shaul told the Colossians that Epaphras was "always laboring earnestly for you in his prayers."(Col.4:12)

Yeshua said, "Come to me, all who are weary and heavy-laden, and I will give you rest. Take my yoke upon you, and learn from me, for I am gentle and humble in heart; and you shall find rest for you souls. For my yoke is easy, and my load is light."(Mt.11:28-30)

He said, "Come to me." We come to Yeshua in prayer. People burn out because they do not come to the Lord. They are trying in their own strength alone. They are running an engine without oil. The friction produces great heat which burns out the engine.

If things are getting you down, and you are growing weary of the continual battle going on and on, what should you do? "Come to me," Yeshua said, "I will give you rest" — rest for your souls. "He leads me beside still waters, He maketh me to lie down in green pastures ..." Shabbat was made for man so that he would remember that God is the source, so that man could have rest.

A talmid is a student. To be a talmid of the Lord, you must be learning from Him. To take His yoke upon you means, as it does for the ox, that you follow your master's leading. When you take His yoke upon you, the sign of ownership, you are acknowledging His Lordship and can learn of Him.

The Lordship of Yeshua cannot be established in your life without prayer. If you do not pray, then he is not your Source. If you do not pray, he is not the one leading and ordering your life. You are.

Humility is simply letting God have His proper place, recognizing your place in His sight, and giving Him the glory He deserves. It is not pretending to be other than who you are, but rather being the one whom the Lord has made you. Humility is not the same as timidity or silence. It is willingly doing what God wants you to do. It is saying "yes" on the inside as well as the outside. Then "you shall find rest for your souls."

If you take his yoke upon you, he will see to it that you accomplish something worthwhile. Supernaturally, he will enable you to pull a load greater than what you could pull in your own strength.

### A Prayer for Talmidim

The talmidim said to Yeshua, "Lord, teach us to pray." He taught them what has come to be known as "the Lord's Prayer." (Mt.6:9-13) Many lives have been changed by what he taught. Many books have been written about it. Let's look at it as a pattern for prayer.

Yeshua said, "When you pray, pray like this: Our Father ..." Why did he say "Our" instead of "My"? Because the New Covenant is a corporate covenant, not an individual covenant. It is a covenant which God made with the house of Israel and the house of Judah, and you are brought into it. "For I am a Father to Israel." (Jer.31:9) You are part of a people God created to bring light to the world. "For this is what the Lord has commanded us, 'I have placed you as light for the

Gentiles, that you should bring yeshuah [salvation] to the end of the earth.'" (Acts 13:47)

You are also an integral part of a body of believers that is spread throughout space and time. We are members of one body. That is important to learn and keep in mind.

Saying "OUR Father" should help you realize that there are other people in this family. We are not told to pray "Give ME this day MY daily bread ..." or "Forgive ME MY debts," or "Lead ME not into temptation ..." or "Deliver ME ...". No, Yeshua said, "Pray ... give US, forgive US, lead US, and deliver US."

Who is this "us" that I am supposed to be praying for? To begin with, the "us" is the others in the covenant — the House of Judah, the House of Israel. It also includes those who have been grafted in. We are to be concerned about others, even others we have not seen or met. We must love those we have seen if we love God whom we have not seen.

"Our Father who art in heaven ..." God is our father who loves us and is concerned about us. He is a perfect father, teaching and disciplining, giving us opportunities to serve and to grow. One day we will see Him as He is and we will be like Him. That is our destiny and our desire.

This world, this life, is not all there is. God dwells in heaven, in eternity, above all. That is His home. It is the present location of our home, too, until the New Yerushalayim comes down. For we are His children, and that is where our citizenship is located. (Phil. 3:20) We should live our lives with our minds and hearts set upon eternal things, the things of the Spirit.

"Our Father, who art in heaven, sanctified be Your Name ..." We are here to sanctify the Name of God by our lives. If we want His Name to be treated as holy, then we must treat it as holy and we must so live that others will see our good works and glorify our Father in heaven.

God said of Israel, "When they came to the nations where they went, they profaned My holy name, because it was said of them, 'These are the people of the Lord; yet they have come out of His land.'" (Ezek.36:20) God had to bring judgment upon His people because of their sins. Before all the world, He had to take them captive out of His land which He had promised to them. The nations where they were scattered mocked them and their God. We must so live that that will not happen in our lives.

Ask yourself what you can do to see that the Name of the Lord is sanctified in and through Israel. What can you do to see that it is sanctified in and through the Kahal? in yourself, your family, your nation, and the world?

"Your kingdom come ..." This world is not our home and it is not what we desire as our home. We want the kingdom of God, which is better, greater, and more wonderful than everything else. There is nothing else that can be compared to it. The kingdom of God is "righteousness, peace, and joy in the Ruakh HaKodesh." (Rom.14:17) Righteousness comes before peace and joy; and those who hunger and thirst for righteousness will be satisfied.

"Your kingdom come, Your will be done ..." Who will do the will of God? someone else? Who will obey the laws and do the work of the kingdom? other people? Hopefully they will, but will you? The Lord establishes His kingdom, but He usually does it through people, especially those who long for His kingdom. Perhaps the talmidim were really asking, "How can we get God to do things for us?" The prayer that Yeshua gave them was not one of getting, but one of commitment to and relationship with the Father.

We are told, "For this is the will of God, your sanctification; that is, that you abstain from sexual immorality; that each of you know how to possess his own vessel in sanctification and honor, not in lustful passion, like the Gentiles who do not know God; and that no man transgress and defraud his brother in the matter because the Lord is the avenger in all these things ..." (1 Thes.4:3-6) This is a world filled with fleshly temptations. If you submit yourself to the Spirit of Holiness, the spirits of lust will not control you.

We are also told that "The Lord is not slow about His promise, as some count slowness, but is patient toward you, not wishing for any to perish but for all to come to repentance." (2 Pet.3:9) For, God "desires all men to be saved and to come to the knowledge of the truth." (1 Tim.2:4) God is patient with you, not only for your salvation, but for the salvation of others. That is the will of God. If you are earnestly praying for it, you will be earnestly living for it.

"Your will be done in EARTH as it is in heaven ..." This earth is not the way it is supposed to be. It is supposed to be obedient to God. Darkness should not be ruling on the earth; light should be. Just as it is in heaven, let it be here upon the earth. One day, it will be. For, "All flesh is grass, and all its loveliness is like the flower of the field. The grass withers, the flower fades, when the breath of the Lord blows upon it; surely the people are grass. The grass withers, the flower fades, but the word of our God stands forever." (Is.40:6-8)

"Give us this day our daily bread ..." As much as this is a prayer for provision, it is also a prayer for dependence. The meaning is, "Give us the bread that we need for today. Tomorrow we will ask You for what we need then." Our natural inclination is to pray, "Give us today our bread for the month, and enough to fill the freezer, refrigerator, and pantry." Yeshua is saying that we should want to be daily dependent upon God. This is not a prayer for abundance, but for a walk of faith with God.

We know that, "Man shall not live by bread alone, but by every word that proceeds from the mouth of God." (Dt.8:3; Mt.4:4) So, we need to hunger for the bread of life. We need to hear from God today. His mercies are new every morning, and so is His guidance and provision.

"Forgive us our debts as we forgive our debtors ..." We should understand that we owe God much more than anyone could ever owe us. Therefore, in humility, we keep unforgiveness far from us. "Forgive us AS we forgive others ..." That will bring judgment to some people, because with what measure you give to others, it will be given to you. We are told, "And be kind to one another, tender-hearted, forgiving each other, just as God in Messiah also has forgiven you." (Eph.4:32)

"Lead us not into temptation ..." We depend upon the Lord, we trust in Him and not our own strength; but are not seeking to put the Lord to the test. We want to be led in His ways, not the ways of temptation. There is a bumper sticker which says, "Lead me not into temptation, I can find it myself." Certainly, those who want to find temptation can find it everywhere. Those who want to avoid and overcome temptation should pray accordingly.

"But deliver us from evil." There is evil in the world, and there is an evil one. He walks about as a roaring lion looking for someone to devour. It needn't be you. Recognize the reality, and don't think yourself invincible. If you didn't need a deliverer, God wouldn't have provided one for you.

"For Yours is the kingdom and the power and the glory, forever." In reminding God, we remind ourselves that all things exist for His purposes and pleasure. Even when we request these things for "us," we are requesting them according to His will, for Him. It is His kingdom that is to be advanced. It is His power which will accomplish it. And He is the one who will receive all the glory from it. He is the King of Glory. The working and establishment of His kingdom in our lives will bring eternal glory to God.

# 5. Commitment to

# GROWTH

When God called Abraham, He promised him, "And I will make you a great nation, and I will bless you, and make your name great; and so you shall be a blessing; ... and in you all the families of the earth shall be blessed." (Gen.12:2,3) God called Abraham when he was a single, insignificant one, but His plan was to make him grow into a great nation.

Abraham walked with God for many years and God blessed him with flocks and herds and great wealth, but he had no children. "After these things, the word of the Lord came to Abram in a vision, saying, 'Do not fear, Abram, I am a shield to you; your very great reward.' And Abram said, 'O Lord God, what will You give me, since I am childless, and the heir of my house is Eliezer of Damascus?' And Abram said, 'Since You have given no offspring to me, one born in my house is my heir.' " (Gen.15:1-3)

In the Lord, Abraham was destined to become great and to become a multitude. God had given him wealth, but no children. Abraham was thankful for the wealth, but not content with it. How could he become a great nation without having any children? How could all the families of the earth be blessed in him if he had no family himself?

Abraham had continual sorrow and pain because, no matter how else God blessed him, he was unable to father a child. There was nothing Abraham could do about it; there was nothing Sarah could do about it either, except to cry out to God. And that is what Abraham did. He did not harden his heart and say, "Oh, I don't care about it anyway." He did not become despondent and bitter. In anguish, he called out to his God who had promised and who was able to fulfill that promise.

I believe that God wanted Abraham to cry out to Him; perhaps He even provoked him to do it. We don't always like to be open and vulnerable, but God wants us to be. He wants us to express and request of Him the deepest desires of our hearts.

"Then behold the word of the Lord came to him, saying, 'This man will not be your heir; but one who shall come forth from your inner parts, he shall be your heir.' And He took him outside and said, 'Now look toward the heavens, and count the stars, if you are able to count them.' And He said to him, 'So shall your descendants be.'" (Gen.15:4,5)

God was saying, "Abraham, from what you truly are deep down inside, there will come forth a child to be your heir." Then God took Abraham outside of his little earthly dwelling to show him how big this whole enterprise really is — as big as the infinite heavens.

Was it important to God? Did He care whether or not Abraham ever grew into a multitude? In all of creation at that time, there was nothing more important than that Abraham grow. The salvation of the world depended upon it.

God is looking for growth. That's why He supernaturally gave Isaac to Abraham and Sarah. That's why He promised to send Messiah. "For a child will be born to us, a son will be given to us; and the government will be on his shoulders; and his name willl be called Wonderful Counselor, Mighty God, Eternal Father,

Prince of Peace. There will be no end to the increase of his government or of peace, on the throne of David and over his kingdom, to establish it and to uphold it with justice and righteousness from then on and forevermore. The zeal of the Lord of hosts will accomplish this." (Is.9:6-7)

Messiah's kingdom continually grows. He is born to Israel, but that is not where his kingdom stops. One day it will fill all of space and time. "... For out of Tzion shall go forth the Law and the word of the Lord from Yerushalayim. And He will judge between the nations, and will render decisions for many peoples; and they will hammer their swords into plowshares, and their spears into pruning hooks. Nation will not lift up sword against nation, and never again will they learn war." (Is.2:3,4)

Every living organism is either in the process of growing or of dying. Those who believe in Yeshua are members of a body that is alive and growing. Therefore, every believer needs to be growing personally, and contributing to the growth of the body. Growth is natural. Into every seed is built the blueprint of what it will become. If you plant vegetable seeds and they don't grow, you'll look for another store that sells good seeds. If a child isn't growing, you take him to the doctor to find out why. Growth is normal.

Yeshua told His talmidim, "I am the vine, you are the branches; he who abides in me, and I in him, he bears much fruit; for apart from me you can do nothing." (Jn.15:5) God intends for each of Abraham's children to grow. Every believer must have a commitment to grow, despite the special pains that growth brings; some physical, some mental, some emotional or spiritual. The very act of growing can make you sore in different places, especially as the Lord cuts away certain parts of your life to ensure the growth of good fruit.

Growth in the Lord, like physical growth, depends a lot on what you eat — "Garbage in, garbage out." A healthy diet includes daily portions of the Scriptures and prayer, and regular fellowship with other believers in a congregation where God's Word is faithfully proclaimed.

Growth in the Lord, as opposed to physical growth, requires effort. Abraham couldn't create his own son, but he could cry out to God. God makes the growth take place, but you must desire to grow, desire to change from what you are to be more like Yeshua. You should hunger and thirst for righteousness and for the Lord Himself.

One of the analogies that describes becoming a believer is being "born anew." Babies are wonderful. Toddlers are cute. The first day of school is exciting. But for the one who has received eternal life, life has no stop signs, not even death. We are to continue to grow and change.

There are some who say they believe, but do not make any effort to grow. Thinking they have gone far enough, they stake their claim, drive in their tent pegs, and start to homestead. But we are not called to seek comfort in this ungodly world. Nor are we called to seek some kind of well-rounded social-spiritual mix, but rather to earnestly desire the coming of God's kingdom. "Woe to those who are at ease in Tzion, and to those who are secure in the mountain of Shomron ..." (Amos 6:1)

God brought the children of Israel out of Egypt to bring them to the land of Israel, but they continued to turn back in their hearts to Egypt. They were unwilling to go on. They refused to believe that they were able, in the Lord, to defeat the giants in the land.

Yehoshua and Caleb pleaded with the people, "and

they spoke to all the congregation of the sons of Israel, saying, 'The land which we passed through to spy out is an exceedingly good land. If the Lord is pleased with us, then He will bring us into this land, and give it to us — a land which flows with milk and honey. Only do not rebel against the Lord; and do not fear the people of the land, for they shall be our prey. Their protection has been removed from them, and the Lord is with us; do not fear them.' But all the congregation said to stone them with stones." (Num.14:7-10) The people were not willing to go and grow in the face of the battle that God had prepared for them. They were, however, willing to stone those who encouraged them to believe God.

There are some things that help an individual and a group to grow. The Book of Proverbs speaks often about being teachable, humble, willing to accept correction and instruction. "He is on the path of life who heeds instruction, but he who forsakes reproof goes astray." (Prov.10:17) Some refuse correction and wander off the path of life.

Yeshua told his talmidim the parable of the talents to teach them to wisely increase whatever had been entrusted to them, be it wealth, ability, or position. That may be hard to do, but we can learn how. A talmid is someone who is learning — a student — someone who is voluntarily under the discipline of the Lord. We do not know all that we need to know. We probably are not doing all that we can do. It is the Lord who teaches and enables us.

Growing in the Lord is really the Lord growing in you. Yochanan the Matbil said, "He must increase, but I must decrease." (Jn.3:30) If you lose your life for his sake and for the message of the kingdom, then you will find your life. As the individual grows, the family, congregation, and kingdom can grow.

God has established certain positions of responsibility to assist that growth. "He gave some as ambassadors, some prophets, and some as heralds of the kingdom message, and some shepherds and teachers for the equipping of those set apart for the work of service, to the building up of the body of the Messiah until we all attain to the unity of the faith and of the knowledge of the Son of God, to a mature man, to the measure of the stature which belongs to the fulness of Messiah. As a result, we are no longer to be children, tossed here and there by waves, and carried about by every wind of doctrine, by the trickery of men, by craftiness in deceitful scheming. But, speaking the truth in love, we are to grow up in all aspects into him who is the head, Messiah, from whom the whole body, being fitted and held together by that which every joint supplies, according to the proper working of each individual part, causes the growth of the body for the building up of itself in love." (Eph.4:11-16)

Speaking the truth in love, we are to grow up in everything into him. This is a challenge. Sometimes we err by speaking the truth, but not in love. Sometimes we err by loving someone, but neglecting to tell them the truth they need to hear. We need to speak the truth in love and be willing to hear the truth spoken to us. Hopefully, it will be spoken to us in love, but nevertheless we need to recognize and receive it. The truth that we give and the truth that we receive help us and others to grow.

The members of a body grow together. It is unusual to have a body where some members, the fingers for example, grow to maturity, while others, the toes, remain in their infancy. Sometimes strange things happen where the endocrine system isn't working, or the pituitary glands are malfunctioning, but that is abnormal. The body of the Lord, although it has older and more mature members, must still grow as a whole. The work of the Lord upon the earth is to be done by His body. Individual believers are to work and grow together.

At any given moment, not everyone will be able to walk on the water, challenge Goliath, or command the sun and the moon to stand still. Nor are we all called to do the same thing, but we are called to mature together. We are members of each other. If one is honored, all are honored; if one suffers, all suffer. If one member of the body is lazy or asleep, the entire body is slowed down. God can bypass people, and He often does, but it is His intention that the entire body become what it is supposed to be. That is why we need to speak the truth in love, correcting each other because we care for each other and for the work of God. "Open rebuke is better than secret love." (Prov.27:5)

Shaul the ambassador had much in his life that could have been a source of personal pride, "However, what things were gain to me, these I have counted loss for Messiah. Yes, most assuredly, and I count all things to be loss for the excellency of the knowledge of Messiah Yeshua, my Lord, for whom I have suffered the loss of all things, and count them as worthless for the purpose of gaining Messiah." (Phil.3:7,8)

To grow, we put away childish things, like the toys and praises of the world. To grow, we set our affection on things above and not on things on the earth. When Yeshua comes for his own, the things of the world, and those who hang onto them, will be left behind. When he establishes the Messianic kingdom, those whose hearts are pure, those whose eyes have a single focus, will fill the earth with good fruit.

Shaul continues, "... And may be found in him, not having a righteousness of my own derived from the

Law, but that which is through faith in Messiah, the righteousness which comes from God on the basis of faith, that I may know him, and the power of his resurrection and the fellowship of his sufferings, being conformed to his death; in order that I may attain to the resurrection from the dead. Not that I have already obtained it, or have already become perfect, but I press on in order that I may lay hold of that for which also I was laid hold of by Messiah Yeshua. Brethren, I do not regard myself as having laid hold of it yet; but one thing I do: forgetting what lies behind and reaching forward to what lies ahead, I press on toward the goal for the prize of the high calling of God in Messiah Yeshua." (Phil.3:10-14)

Shaul, an ambassador of the Lord, said, 'I press on. There's more to attain. I must continue to change and grow. I have not yet attained.' It is true that only the Lord can do it — it is GOD who gives the increase — but the Lord will give the increase in response to the fervent desire of a heart. If a person makes no effort to change, and goes his own way expecting that God will change him without his participation, he will be disappointed. Likewise, if he refuses to believe that he needs to change, his whole life will be a disappointment.

"All discipline for the moment seems not to be joyful, but sorrowful; yet to those who have been trained by it, afterwards it yields the peaceful fruit of righteousness." (Heb.12:11) Being disciplined by the Lord is not fun, but it trains you and makes you fruitful. God is a Father who disciplines all who are truly His children, so that they will grow. He disciplines us because we are not already all that we need to be.

The distance between what we are and what He is making us is very great. We read of the tragedy of some believers, "For though by this time you ought to be teachers, you have need again for someone to teach you the elementary principles of the oracles of God, and you have come to need milk and not solid food. For everyone who partakes only of milk is not accustomed to the word of righteousness, for he is a babe. But solid food is for the mature, who because of practice have their senses trained to discern good and evil." (Heb.5:12-14)

Because they weren't willing to be trained, they were still babies. Others drifted away, because they neglected the things of God. Shaul said, "I therefore run in this way, not with uncertainty. I fight in this way, as not beating the air, but I press down my body and bring it into submission, lest by any means, after I have proclaimed to others, I myself should be rejected." (1Co.9:26,27)

God has placed ambassadors, prophets, heralds, shepherds and teachers in the congregational structure to help believers grow. They are not perfect; they are growing, too; but God has given them to the congregation so that the congregation can grow. That is His plan and procedure. People who reject God's plan for their own growth have a hard time growing. They drift away. Unless it is physically impossible, every believer should be a committed member of a local congregation. It is pride and unbelief that keep some people from submitting to the Lord's authority that He has entrusted to fallible human beings.

To grow in all things, we die to the past and grow into the future, which is eternal. We press on because we have no other identity, gods, or desires. As we grow, we give up what needs to go and develop whatever needs to be developed. We develop the ability to hear the voice of the Lord, and to speak for Him. We begin to see that we are talmidim, students in lifelong learning, taking an active role in our own education and training.

"Lord, let's work on this problem in my life. Show me the right way to do it. Make me a workman who knows how to use his tools."

God gives us the understanding, the growth, and the fruit as we abide in Him, but we make the choice in our hearts. "When we see him we will be like him for we shall see him as He is. And everyone who has this hope purifies himself even as he (Yeshua) is pure." (1Jn.3:3) If you want to see the Lord and be like Him, you will work to purify yourself, choosing the Lord and His discipline. Your heart's cry, like that of Abraham, should be for fruit in your life — spiritual growth and the privilege of bringing other souls into God's kingdom.

# 6. Commitment to

# THE COVENANT

"Now when Abram was ninety-nine years old, the Lord appeared to Abram and said to him, 'I am God Almighty; walk before Me, and be complete. And I will give My covenant between Me and you, and I will multiply you exceedingly. ...This is My covenant, which you shall keep, between Me and you and your seed after you: every male among you shall be circumcised. And you shall be circumcised in the flesh of your foreskin; and it shall be the sign of the covenant between Me and you.'"(Gen.17:1-2,10-11)

Abraham had a covenant relationship with God. God initiated the covenant and told Abraham and his children to keep it. At the same time, God changed Abram's name to Abraham, making him the father of the Jewish people, and declaring that he would also become the father of a multitude of Gentiles (cf. verse 5).

The covenant provided a framework for Abraham's relationship with God. The relationship had been established first.

Abraham did exactly what God had told him to do, because he understood the importance of the covenant. "In the very same day Abraham was circumcised, and Ishmael his son. And all the men of his household, who were born in the house or bought with money from a foreigner, were circumcised with him." (Gen.17:26-27)

Just as God framed His relationship with Abraham

through a covenant, so He also did with Israel at Sinai through the covenant of the Law. God's relationship with Israel was established when He chose Abraham, but the covenant gave it specific form.

"So Moses took the blood and sprinkled it on on the people, and said, 'Behold the blood of the covenant, which the Lord has cut with you in accordance with all these words.'"(Ex.24:8) A covenant is "cut," not "made," because it is sealed by a sacrificial death.

God's relationship with Israel had been established through Abraham, long before Sinai. God redeemed us from Egypt before He brought us to Sinai. He showed His power and His goodness to us, but we failed to keep the covenant of the Law. Generation after generation, we failed. To reaffirm and further His relationship with Israel, God promised to establish a New Covenant.

Jeremiah 31:31-34 presents the outline of the New Covenant. (Ezekiel 36 gives a similar presentation, in somewhat different language, of the same conditions of the New Covenant.) "'Behold, the days come,' says the Lord, 'that I will cut with the house of Israel and with the house of Judah a new covenant, not like the covenant that I cut with their fathers in the day I took them by their hand to bring them out from the land of Egypt, which they broke, My covenant, although I was a husband to them,' says the Lord.

"'But this is the covenant that I will cut with the house of Israel after those days,' says the Lord. 'I will put My law in their inward parts and upon their heart I will write it; and I will be to them for God, and they will be to Me for a people. And they will not again teach each man his neighbor and each man his brother saying, "Know the Lord!" for all of them will know Me from their least even to their greatest,' says the Lord, for I will forgive their iniquities and their sins I will not remember again.'"(Jer.31:31-34)

The Lord promised to remove the stony heart of His people and replace it with a heart of flesh. This "circumcision of the heart" was necessary to remove its hardness, stubbornness, and rebellion. That is why it was necessary for God to promise: "I will put My Spirit within you and cause you to walk in My statutes, and you will be careful to observe My ordinances." (Ezek.36:27)

Israel, God's chosen people, had been living an ungodly, though often religious, existence, without God and in defiance of God. "And I spoke to you, rising up early and speaking, but you did not hear, and I called you but you did not answer. ...Since the day that your fathers came out of the land of Egypt until this day, I have sent you all My servants the prophets, daily rising early and sending them. Yet they did not listen to Me or incline their ear, but stiffened their neck; they did evil more than their fathers." (Jer.7:13,25-26)

He told Ezekiel, "'Therefore, say to the house of Israel, 'Thus says the Lord God, "It is not for your sake, O house of Israel, that I am about to act, but for My holy name, which you have profaned among the nations where you went." (Ezek.36:22)

God had placed His Name on Israel, but Israel was unfaithful, breaking the covenant. In His mercy, and for the sake of His own Name, God promised to make a New Covenant to replace the covenant of the Law. This New Covenant is related to, but different from the one it replaces. It is not simply a renewal of the covenant of the Law. In what way is it the same? In what way is it different?

There are five important aspects of the New Covenant. Knowing them will better enable us to keep the covenant, just as knowing the conditions and requirements of a certain job — its rules and regulations, pay and benefits — will better enable us to do that job. 1) The New Covenant is a corporate covenant. 2) It is a Jewish covenant. 3) It is written on our hearts. 4) It enables us to know God through a living relationship with Him. 5) It brings us forgiveness.

**1) A Corporate Covenant:** "I will make a New Covenant with the house of Israel and the house of Judah." This is not a covenant between God and an individual, but between God and the "house" of Israel and the "house" of Judah. It is a corporate covenant, not an individual one like Abraham or David had. Why is it with the "house"? Because God has been looking, since the beginning of creation, for a people, gathered together in a covenant relationship with Him, to worship Him in spirit and in truth. He created Israel to be that people.

**2) A Jewish Covenant:** Since this covenant is cut with the house of Israel and the house of Judah, it is a Jewish covenant. When God spoke to Jeremiah, the house of Israel, including Ezekiel, was already in exile in Babylon. The house of Judah was still in the land, but about to be removed. In stating that this covenant would be with both houses, God was affirming His intention to restore both. In then stating that it would be with the house of Israel, God is looking to the day when all Israel is again made one.

The distinction between those Jews who entered into the New Covenant and those who did not was not a physical or outward one — what they ate or how they dressed — it was a distinction in heart alone. God circumcised the hearts of those Jews who believed. Because all Israel did not believe, salvation through the New Covenant also became available to the Gentiles. (Rom.11:11,30) The Gentiles who believed were grafted into the commonwealth of Israel. God circumcised their hearts. Commitment to a covenant made with the house of Israel and the house of Judah necessarily implies a commitment to Israel and the Jewish people.

Israel was created to be a holy people, to represent God in the earth, and to be a light to all the nations. God has always kept a remnant in Israel faithful to Himself. He intends to dwell in the midst of a wholly redeemed Israel, and to establish His kingdom on earth, centered in Jerusalem, over all the peoples.

It is the Kahal — the commonwealth and community of Israel — that provides the context for the kingdom of God. Individual Gentiles, without becoming Jews, can become part of the Kahal of Israel by choosing to accept the rule of Messiah, the King of the Jews. Within the one Messianic body, there are different members with different functions and callings.

**3) Written upon Hearts:** "My law I will put within them, and on their heart I will write it." The covenant of the Law given at Sinai was engraved on tablets of stone; the New Covenant is engraved on the internal tablets of the heart. The Law demonstrated God's holiness, righteousness, and goodness. Obeying it would have trained Israel to keep the two great commandments, to "love the Lord your God with all of your heart, with all your soul, and with all your might" (Dt.6:5), and to "love your neighbor as yourself." (Lev.19:18) For, as Yeshua said, "On these depend all the Law and the Prophets." (Mt.22:39-40)

God's law is perfect, but man's will and actions are not. Israel did not, and could not, keep it. The problem with the covenant of the Law was not with God's law, but with sinful human nature. The Law tells us to love our neighbor, but we often choose not to.

"Love does no wrong to a neighbor; love therefore is

the fulfillment of the Law." (Rom.13:10) In the New Covenant, this reality is engraved on our hearts. The heart pumps blood throughout the body. God's law is written upon our hearts to be the life that flows through our whole being.

God puts His Law and His Spirit within us so that we will be a clean and lawful people; not in external show, nor distorted by the traditions of men, but as the fruit of that internal life that flows through us. God's purity and holiness is to be the source and sustenance of the life that we live before God and men.

**4) A Living Relationship:** "I will be their God, and they will be My people ... for they shall all know Me." The Lord spoke of "Abraham My friend" (Is.41:8). The children of Abraham should have that same close relationship with the God of Abraham. Through the New Covenant, we can.

This New Covenant relationship with God is both a great privilege and a great responsibility. It gives personal access to His presence, His wisdom, and His love. It requires that we live accordingly. In the New Covenant, every individual is responsible for finding out from God what to do, and then doing it. Others can help us, but the responsibility rests with the individual.

"I will be their God" means 'I am the One they are to worship, serve, and fear. I am the One who will protect and provide for them.' In the New Covenant, we are called to trust God always and continually; to depend ultimately upon Him and not upon ourselves, or someone or something else.

Since people do not want to be vulnerable, they often put on their own armour, build their own fortresses, and mount their own guards on the towers. But we are promised that, "He who keeps Israel neither slumbers nor sleeps." (Ps.121:4) God is the Protector who is always there. Though His ways are not our ways, we need to trust Him. Sometimes we will not understand, but His ways are always much higher than ours. (Is.55:8,9)

"They shall be My people." The God of Israel is not like the patron gods or saints of the ancient world who had only their own people or territory that they protected. He is the God of all the earth. He is the one true God, yet He has a people. Though all the earth is His, He has a land. This people is composed of the house of Israel, the house of Judah, and those who, like Ruth and Rahab, join themselves to this people. God will bring the Gentiles into a holy relationship with Himself, into the commonwealth of Israel.

**5) "For I will forgive their iniquity and their sin I shall remember no more."** Iniquity is the evil way within us, the something in the very nature of man that causes him to be wrong — to be wrong-headed, wrong-hearted, wrong-wayed. People can and must choose between what is good and what is evil, but there is something in our nature that inclines us to what is evil, to what is self-centered rather than to what is God-centered.

Before the flood, "The Lord saw that the wickedness of man was great on the earth, and that every intent [יצר] of the thoughts of his heart was only evil continually." (Gen.6:5) After the flood: "And the Lord said to His heart, 'I will never again curse the ground on account of man, for the intent [יצר] of man's heart is evil from his youth; and I will never again destroy every living thing, as I have done.'" (Gen.8:21)

After waiting forty years for the rebellious generation that he led out of Egypt to die in the wilderness, Moses prophesied of the continuing future rebellion of Israel and the judgments of God that it would bring. At the end of this "Song of Moses," the Lord says: "Then it shall come about, when many evils and troubles have come upon them, that this song will testify before them as a witness (for it shall not be forgotten from the lips of their descendants); for I know their intent [יצר] which they are making today, before I have brought them into the land which I swore." (Dt.32:21) God saw their evil intent and made it clear that He had warned them in advance.

In the New Covenant, God provides forgiveness for the iniquity that causes man to veer off to the right or the left instead of going straight ahead. He forgives what we cannot change. Then He puts His own Spirit within us to enable us to change.

"Their sin I will remember no more." The Levitical system, which was the center of the covenant of the Law, required continual sacrifices; morning and evening, on holy days, and especially on Yom Kippur, the Day of Atonement. With the New Covenant, that is no longer the case. The sacrificial death of Messiah is sufficient to atone for all sin.

Our sins are atoned for and God casts them all into the depths of the sea. (Mic.7:19) God opens our eyes so that we can see our sin and iniquity, but He will not reproach us for the past. Once we have acknowledged a sin, repented of it, made restitution for it, or whatever else might be necessary, we receive the forgiveness of the Lord and go on. We don't carry the weight of the past around with us forever.

So, there are these five important distinctions of the New Covenant: 1) It is a corporate covenant; not just you and God. 2) It is a Jewish covenant, into which Jews enter and Gentiles may be grafted by faith. 3) God's eternal Law is written on our hearts, rather than on tablets of stone. It changes our nature. 4) It establishes a living relationship with God whereby we know Him.

5) Our iniquity is forgiven and our sin is forgotten, atoned for by the once-for-all sacrifice of Yeshua the Messiah.

# 7. Commitment to

# MAKE TALMIDIM

"And Abram took Sarai his wife and Lot his nephew, and all their possessions which they had accumulated, and the persons which they had acquired in Haran, and they set out for the land of Canaan; thus they came into the land of Canaan." (Gen.12:5) Literally, Abram and Sarai took with them, "the souls which they had made in Haran."

"The Rabbis take the word 'souls' to mean the proselytes whom Abram made among the men, and Sarai among the women. These converts became subservient to God's law and followed their master in his spiritual adventure."[1] Rashi, a renowned medieval Jewish commentator, says, "The text indicates that Abraham had brought them in under the wings of the Divine Presence. Abraham proselytized the men and Sarah proselytized the women. And the verse credits them as though they had made them; therefore, it is written, 'which they had made.'"[2]

Abraham knew the Lord and wanted others to know Him too. Making talmidim is the act of bringing others to the knowledge of God and His kingdom, and then helping them to live in the light of it. It is a natural consequence of knowing the Lord.

From Abraham, God created a people, Israel, to know Him and serve Him. Because God revealed Himself to Israel, He expected that Israel would reveal Him to the Gentiles. From the beginning, it was the purpose of God that His message should go forth to all the earth that all men might know and serve Him. The children of Israel were the ones whom God designed for that purpose.

From the beginning, God had a plan for reconciling the world to Himself. "And the Scripture, foreseeing that God would justify the Gentiles by faith, proclaimed the message of the kingdom beforehand to Abraham, saying 'All the nations will be blessed in you.'" (Gal. 3:8) That blessing would come from receiving the knowledge of God. The prophets envisioned the day in which all the earth will be filled with the glory of the Lord as the waters cover the sea.

In order to bring the message of the kingdom to others, you must first receive, believe, and live it yourself. That is why God continually sent prophets to Israel with a call for repentance. Israel will be a pure light to the nations when that call is answered.

Isaiah 52:13-53:15 is a clear prophetic picture of the Messiah despised and rejected of men, but bringing atonement. The prophecy is preceded by the declaration: "How lovely on the mountains are the feet of him who brings good news, who announces peace and brings the kingdom message of happiness, who announces salvation, and says to Tzion, 'Your God reigns!'" (Is.52:7)

Israel must hear the kingdom message of salvation in God her King. For as we are reminded by Shaul, a Pharisee of Pharisees — one who received the kingdom message — "How then shall they call upon him in whom they have not believed? And how shall they believe in him of whom they have not heard? And how shall they hear without someone proclaiming? And how shall they proclaim unless they are sent?" (Rom.10:14-15) Israel, having heard and received, is to proclaim the message to the Gentiles.

The Greek word, *euangelion*, sometimes translated as "good news" was used in particular for the good report that an enemy was overcome on the battlefield." A runner was sent from the battle to proclaim the victory that had been won, the advancement of the kingdom. At the time of Absalom's revolt against King David, "Ahimaaz the son of Zadok said, 'Please let me run and bring the king news that the Lord has freed him from the hand of his enemies. ... And the watchman [who saw him coming] said, 'I think the running ... is like the running of Ahimaaz the son of Zadok.' And the king said, 'This is a good man and comes with good news.'" (2 Sam.18:19,27)

The ambassador, i.e. *shaliakh*, Shaul said he was called by Yeshua "that I might proclaim his message of the kingdom among the Gentiles...." (Gal.1:16) Yeshua is the king. To tell of his victory over sin, self, death, and darkness is to proclaim the message of the kingdom. In Hebrew, his name means "victory," as well as "salvation," "healing," and "deliverance." The victory in him is eternal.

Ever since Adam rebelled against the Lord, there has been a war going on. Because of Adam's rebellion, all his children have been taken captive by the enemy. When Yeshua was crucified and raised from the dead, he overcame all the power of the enemy; he was empowered to set the captives free. In the battle for your eternal soul, as well as for the souls of all men, only Yeshua has won the victory.

Who is the enemy? There are several: temptation, sin, death, and the Accuser. It is the desires of the flesh and the ways of the world that ensnare people — "the lust of the eyes, the lust of the flesh, and the boastful pride of life." (1 Jn.2:16) These are powerful enemies, but Yeshua has defeated them.

In some wars, the fighting continues after the war is officially over. There remain "pockets of resistance" that need to be destroyed. The war is over, but the fighting continues. Ten, twenty, thirty, forty years after the end of World War II, on small Pacific islands, Japanese soldiers were still discovered in hiding, or sometimes they gave themselves up. The enemies that you face have been defeated, but that does not mean that they can no longer attack; that does not mean that they can no longer inflict damage. They will attack, and believers need to know how to resist them and how to enforce Yeshua's victory.

The Greek word *kerusso*, for "herald" or proclaimer, was used to signify the messenger who was sent to an enemy city to demand its surrender. He represented and bore the authority of his lord, but he went alone without an army. Usually, the herald was heard, and then sent back with a message of surrender or war. Sometimes the herald was mistreated or killed, which brought the wrath of the lord who sent him against that city, as though they had abused the lord himself.

All of this provides a context for understanding and proclaiming the kingdom message, no matter what the cost. We do not represent an earthly power or kingdom. We do not threaten with physical weapons and human armies. In humility and vulnerability, we proclaim the coming kingdom of God.

Abraham brought others to God. His children do the same. By the fruit of our lips and the fruit of our lives, we communicate the kingdom message to others. How they respond to it and to us is their decision.

The call of Yeshua to His talmidim was, and remains, "Follow Me, and I will make you fishers of men."(Mt.4:19) The Greek word used in the Messianic Writings for "fishers" is the same word that is used in the Septuagint in Jeremiah 16:16-17: "'Behold, I will send [*apostello*] many fishers,' says the Lord, 'and they will fish them; and afterward I will send many hunters, and they will hunt them upon every mountain, and upon every hill, and out of the holes of the rocks. For My eyes are upon all their ways; and their iniquities have not been hidden from My eyes.'"

God knows the iniquity of Israel, and of all men and nations. The message of the kingdom of God, brought by the fishermen whom He sends, offers everyone a way to escape what is to come.

For believers, that should provide even more incentive for proclaiming the message of the kingdom. We must obey the Lord, and we must care about those who have no other means of escape. Yeshua commanded, "Go into all the world and proclaim the message of the kingdom to all creation." (Mk.16:15) We are to tell everyone, even though most will not listen. That is their choice — to obey or to disobey the message. We must choose to obey by telling them.

Yeshua commanded his Jewish talmidim that, "repentance for forgiveness of sins should be proclaimed in his name to all the Gentiles, beginning from Yerushalayim." (Lk. 24:47) Those who have received the mercy and forgiveness of the Lord are to offer that mercy and forgiveness to others. Gentiles who believe are specifically told of their obligation to unbelieving Israel: "For as you in time past were disobedient to God, but now have obtained mercy through their disobedience, even so these also have now been disobedient, so that through the mercy shown to you they also may obtain mercy." (Rom.11:30-31)

The greatest of all the commandments is, "Hear O Israel, the Lord our God is one Lord. You shall love the Lord your God with all your heart, soul, strength, and mind." The second that is like unto it is, "You shall love your neighbor as yourself." The Great Commission — "Go into all the world and proclaim the kingdom message" — is the outworking of these two. We cannot love God whom we have not seen if we do not love our neighbor whom we have seen. Love for our neighbor motivates us to proclaim the message of the kingdom.

For some, the words of the kingdom message will be salvation, deliverance, healing, and redemption — life itself. For others, those same words will be witnesses against them on the Day of Judgment. Each individual must choose for himself or herself, but our responsibility is to enable them to make an informed choice, and to pray that they will make the right choice.

For them to understand how good the message of the kingdom is, they need to understand how bad the condition of man is. God tells us truthfully that, "The heart is more deceitful than all else and is desperately sick; who can know it? I, the Lord, search the heart — I test the mind — even to give to each man according to his ways, according to the fruit of his deeds." (Jer.17:9-10)

Man without God is sick, alienated from himself, not knowing who he is, why he is, or how he should live. He is alienated from everyone around him, and most of all from God. God is never fooled by appearances. He sees the hearts and He knows the thoughts. All men are guilty and condemned before a Holy, Holy, Holy God. That is why the message is, "Repent and believe. Turn away from your wicked ways."

When a man says, "I'll do it MY way," he is in grave trouble. God gives each of us light so that we might walk in it. If we reject the light, we have chosen darkness. When we stand before God, He'll simply say, "Continue on, as you have chosen, into that total, outer darkness where there is eternal torment, weeping and gnashing of teeth."

Everyone is without excuse, for even, "The heavens declare the glory of God and the earth shows His handiwork." (Ps.19:1) Anyone who wants to hear can hear., though often we don't hear until the second, or fifty-second, time. God speaks to every heart that is open to listen. He says that the natural condition of man is a sickness unto death; but it can be healed. The condition of man is hopeless, BUT God has entered into human history to become our Hope.

This is central to our message. Sin is terminal, but there is a cure for it. Yeshua became sin on the *tzelav*, and so sin itself was put to death. If we are crucified with him, then our sin and our self-will have already had their way with us unto death. We were found guilty and put to death. We cannot be put in "double jeopardy," i.e., tried twice for the same crime. When we stand before God, we do not need to lie and say, "I didn't do it." We say, "I did do it, but Yeshua paid the penalty for me, and I am crucified in Him." God's justice is satisfied.

Death is overcome by the resurrection. Yeshua rose from the dead. The same God who created life has overcome death, which entered into the world when man rebelled against Him. Now there is hope, now there is life. In Yeshua, the Hope of Israel, God gives us the power to do what is right. In the New Covenant He says, "I will place My Spirit within you." That Spirit gives us the power to live clean, holy lives — set apart for God — lives of righteousness and humility.

By the grace of God, we can do that. As we stay humble before Him, we continue to receive His grace, because "God resists the proud, but gives grace to the humble." (Jacob 4:6)

Yeshua said, "All power, all authority, in heaven and earth has been given to me; therefore, go into all the world and make talmidim of all the Gentiles ... teaching them to observe all that I commanded you ..." (Mt.28:19,20) As we continually learn of him, we should continually be making talmidim, i.e., students, of all the nations; others who will continue to learn of King Yeshua the Messiah.

Sometimes portions of the Bible, like the descriptions of the Tabernacle and its material — every board, clasp, loop, and hook — can seem quite dull. But every object and detail was necessary for the place where the glory of God dwelt. Without each little part, the whole would not have held together, and the glory of God would not have dwelt there.

There is much in life that seems neither glorious nor exciting. Still, whatever is done unto the Lord, no matter how insignificant, will one day be filled with His glory. When the glory of God falls upon a grain of sand, a drop of water, or a routine task, there is nothing more glorious. Even so, God can use the ordinary circumstances of your life to change you and to bring others to glory.

Yeshua said, "The harvest is plentiful, but the workers are few. Therefore beseech the Lord of the harvest to send out workers into His harvest." (Mt. 9:37-38) There are many souls waiting to be brought into God's kingdom, but so few workers. Workers are those who are living a disciplined life, in all its small details, for the glory of God. They are ready, willing and able to work, or to learn if they don't know how.

Moments before he ascended into heaven, Yeshua told the talmidim who had stayed with Him, "You shall receive power when the Ruakh HaKodesh has come upon you, and you shall be my witnesses both in Yerushalayim and Judea, and Shomron and unto the farthest parts of the earth." (Acts 1:8) It is this power from on high that cleanses us, encourages us, and brings the message of the kingdom into the hearts of others. It is this same Spirit of Holiness that enables us to proclaim that there is a savior who has overcome sin, death, and hell itself; to tell others that they might hear and believe. It is God's Spirit that enables us to be talmidim and to make talmidim.

The King will be returning to establish his kingdom upon the earth. It is a kingdom whose law is just and true, whose rulers are righteous. All the kingdoms of this world will be destroyed before it. We are to prepare citizens for a kingdom that is close at hand.

1. The Pentateuch and Haftorahs, J.H. Hertz, Soncino Press, London, 1956, P.46
2. Pentateuch and Rashi's Commentary, Genesis, S.S. & R. Publishing Co., Brooklyn, 1949, P.103

# 8. Commitment to FAMILY

Before Abraham had any children, God chose him and said, "I will make you a father of many nations." He promised him, "In you all the families of the earth will be blessed." Family was very important to Abraham, even when he didn't have one of his own. God chose him to be the father of the Jewish people and of all who believe.

Lot came with his uncle Abraham to the land of Canaan. When Lot's servants quarreled with Abraham's about the limited pastureland, Abraham let his nephew choose whichever part of the land he wanted. Lot picked the best, the watered plain, for himself. In that plain were the cities of Sedom and Amorrah.

Lot faced his tent towards Sedom, so that he saw it every morning when he stepped outside. It became the focus of his thoughts. Eventually, Lot moved to Sedom.

When the king of Sedom was defeated in battle, Lot, his family, and his flocks were taken captive by the victors. When Abraham heard what had happened, he went to deliver him. His nephew had been ungrateful and selfish, and had brought the trouble upon himself, but that didn't lessen Abraham's commitment to him.

Abraham "led out his trained men, born in his house, three hundred and eighteen, and went and pursued as far as Dan ... And he brought back all the goods, and also brought back his kinsman Lot with his possessions, and also the women, and the people."(Gen.14:14,16) Abraham had trained men (literally, "consecrated ones") in his house because he had trained them.

Abraham lived a disciplined life, and disciplined the members of his household. Abraham's heart was always towards his family. When he had no children, his cry was, "Lord, you've given me great wealth, but what does it matter since I have no children?" (Cf. Gen.15:2) It is this very concern for family that suitably characterizes him as the father of the Jewish people, and the father of all those who believe. Even before Isaac was born, the Lord said of Abraham, "I have known him, in order that he may command his children and his household after him to keep the way of the Lord by doing righteousness and justice; in order that the Lord may bring upon Abraham what He has spoken about him." (Gen.18:19)

"This attitude of the Father of the Jewish people towards the child, that it is the highest of human treasures, has remained that of his descendants to the present day. Among the most enlightened nations of antiquity, the child had no rights, no protection, no dignity of any sort. In Greece, for example, weak children were generally exposed on a lonely mountain to perish. The Roman historian (Tacitus) deemed it a contemptible prejudice of the Jews that 'it is a crime among them to kill any child!'" [1]

For those who are truly Abraham's children, every member of their family is precious, no matter how young or old, how big or small. Abraham's fatherhood and father's heart represent God, who is a Father to Israel, and "the God of all the earth." (Is.54:5) This is why God said that all the families of the earth would be blessed in Abraham, rather than just all the "people," "tribes," or "ethnic people-groups." Ultimately, God is raising a family. Adam was created to be a son of God. Though Adam rebelled, God still longed for him with a father's heart, and for all of Adam's descendants. Israel also was created to be a son of God. (cf. Ex.4:22)

Yeshua, the perfectly obedient son, came to gather God's family. When we individually come into a relationship with him, we become God's children. "But as many as received him, to them he gave the right to become children of God, to those who believe in his name." (Jn.1:12) "For it was fitting for Him [God], for whom are all things, and through whom are all things, in bringing many sons to glory, to perfect the author of their salvation through sufferings."(Heb.2:10)

The story of the prodigal son (Luke 15) represents the longing of the father's heart for the son who has gone astray and is wasting his inheritance and his life. When the son comes to his senses, he realizes that his greatest blessing, meaning, and purpose was to be in his father's household. There are restrictions, of course, when we are under the authority of God our Father, but they simply keep us from the way that leads to death.

God has given us earthly families. He created the family. It is the first, most basic, and most essential human institution. Commitment to God enables us to be committed to the family that God has given us.

God created Adam. Out of Adam He created Eve. From Adam and Eve He created children. The members of a family are made of the same stuff — related to, dependent upon, and responsible for one another. That is what makes the sin of Cain so evil. God's question was, "Where is Abel, your brother?" Cain's response was, "Am I my brother's keeper?" — i.e., 'Am I supposed to be concerned about my brother?' Cain was denying the commitment and the concern for his brother's well-being which are the essence of the family.

The family was created before any other human institution. So the mutual commitment of husband and wife, parents and children, brothers and sisters, are primary, essential commitments. The very words — "husband," "wife," "brother," "sister" — indicate a close, loving relationship, though the actual relationships people establish often fall far short of what they should be. This applies to the family into which you were born, the family that you begin if you get married, and the family of Abraham, the friend of God.

The greatest commandment of all is, "Hear O Israel, the Lord our God, the Lord is ONE. And you shall love the Lord your God with all your heart, soul, strength and mind..." That is the individual commitment, which is then followed by the family commitment: "And these words which I command you this day shall be upon your heart, and you shall teach them diligently to your children and shall speak of them when you sit in your house, and when you walk by the way and when you lie down and when you rise up. And you shall bind them for a sign upon your hands and they shall be as frontlets between your eyes. And you shall write them upon the doorposts of your house and upon your gates." (Dt.6:4-9)

This is the most beautiful plan for making talmidim of the kingdom of God. It speaks of the family's commitment to God and to each other. Parents have the responsibility to make God's words a continual part of the everyday life of their children. They can only do that if God's words are a continual part of their own everyday life.

The second commandment, which is like the first, is "You shall love your neighbor as yourself." (Lev.19:18) In the family, we find our closest neighbors. Part of the purpose of the genealogies in the Bible is to teach us that an individual is not just on his own, but is related to others, bears a family name, and represents that family. What one does affects the others, for better or for worse.

God's love for a person means that He also loves that person's children. "The LORD did not set His affection on you and choose you because you were more numerous than other peoples, for you were the fewest of all peoples. But it was because the LORD loved you and kept the oath He swore to your forefathers that He brought you out with a mighty hand and redeemed you from the land of slavery, from the power of Pharaoh king of Egypt. Know therefore that the Lord your God, He is God, the faithful God, who keeps the covenant and the lovingkindness to a thousand generations with those who love Him and keep His commandments." (Dt.7:7-9)

## The Family in the New Covenant

The importance that God places on the family is not diminished in the New Covenant. In fact, the proving ground for New Covenant responsibility is the family. Shaul wrote to Timothy about the appointment of an elder, overseer, or servant in the congregation: "He must be one who manages his own household well, keeping his children under control with all dignity. But if a man does not know how to manage his own household, how will he take care of the congregation of God?" (1 Tim.3:4,5,12) Likewise, the commandment, "Honor your father and your mother, that your days may be prolonged in the land which the Lord your God gives you," is emphasized in the Messianic Writings. (Ex.20:12; Eph.6:1-2; Col.3:20)

The family is the first responsibility for husbands, fathers, wives, mothers, and children. If someone is failing in that first responsibility which God has given, he is not to be given more and greater responsibility. Let a man first be found faithful in the responsibility he has. We do not neglect the work of the Lord by serving our families; our families are part of the work of the Lord. As with everything, we serve them as we serve the Lord.

People have taken out of context and greatly misinterpreted two statements of Yeshua which concern the family. The first is, "If anyone comes to me and does not hate his father and mother, his wife and children, his brothers and sisters — yes, even his own life — he cannot be my talmid. Anyone who does not carry his *tzelav* and follow me cannot be my talmid." (Luke 14:26-27)

Is he telling me to hate my family? Is he telling me to hate my own life? Not exactly. What he means can be seen in the sentence that follows — "And anyone who does not carry his *tzelav* and follow me cannot be my talmid."

Following Yeshua will bring rejection and condemnation. That rejection and condemnation may come from the State; it may come from the religious authorities. It may come from the people we love most. If a person is not willing to accept that, he cannot walk with Yeshua. "He who loves father or mother more than me is not worthy of me; and he who loves son or daughter more than me is not worthy of me." (Mt.10:37)

There can be no love or commitment greater than that to Yeshua. Families sometimes want or demand something that would require disobedience to God. That we cannot do, because we must obey the Lord. It is, however, our love for the Lord that enables us, and requires us, to love our families.

To follow Yeshua, I must hate even my own life. What does that mean? It means that I must recognize that even within myself there are desires and tendencies that lead me in the wrong direction. Unless it is submitted to God, my own life will kill me.

"If anyone would come after me, he must deny himself and take up his *tzelav* and follow me. For whoever wants to save his life will lose it, but whoever loses his life for me and for the message of the kingdom will save it." (Mark 8:34-35) It is only by dying to my own conception of who I am, and by surrendering ownership of my life, that I can truly live.

It is the same with my family. It is only by dying to things as they are that I can find in Yeshua what these relationships truly should be. If I give up my family for him, I will find my family through him.

In Philippi, Shaul and Sila were in jail. God sent an earthquake, the jailer rushed in, fell down, and said to them, "What must I do to be saved?" The answer to his question was, "Believe on the Lord Yeshua the Messiah and you and your household will be saved." (Acts 16:22-34)

Shaul looked at him and saw more than just an unattached individual. He saw a family. The jailer worked at night and slept during the day. Maybe that caused family problems for him; we don't know. But when the man surrendered to the Lord, he received a promise for his household as well as for himself. Your family is part of you, physically and emotionally, and, in God's plan, spiritually too. For a father to love God, he must love his own children. For a husband to love God, he must love his wife.

Particular family responsibilities change over time as one becomes an adult, gets married, has children, etc. The responsibilities change, but the preeminence of the responsibility remains the same. To proclaim the love of God for all people, you must first show it to your own family. "But if anyone does not provide for his own, and especially for those of his household, he has denied the faith and is worse than an unbeliever." (1 Tim. 5:8) Yeshua asked, "For what is a man profited if he gains the whole world and loses or forfeits his soul?" (Lk.9:25) We might also ask, "What will it profit a man if he gains the whole world and loses those closest to him?"

The mother of an internationally known speaker was seriously sick, but he was scheduled to be far away at a series of meetings. He first arranged for someone else to speak in his place, and then called those who had invited him to say, "My mother is very sick. I'm sorry, I can't come, but I have arranged for someone else to speak in my place." The people were very disappointed, "But we want YOU. We've advertised for YOU. We're expecting to hear from God through YOU." He said, "I'm sorry. You can get another speaker, but my mother can't get another son!"

### The Family of Believers

That brings us to the second statement which Yeshua made concerning family that is often misinterpreted. The family of Yeshua, his mother and his brothers, came to take custody of him. "And someone said to Him, 'Behold, your mother and your brothers are standing outside seeking to speak to you.' But he answered the one who was telling him and said, 'Who is my mother, and who are my brothers?' And stretching out his hand toward his talmidim, he said, 'Behold, my mother and my brothers! For whoever does the will of my Father who is in heaven, he is my brother and sister and mother.'"(Mt.12:47-50)

Commitment to family becomes the natural, preordained analogy for commitment to the Kahal, the household of God. We are to be concerned for others, their needs, and their responsibilities, regardless of whether or not it brings us any visible benefit, reward, or reciprocity. We are called to do the will of God, and will receive more than we deserve from Him for all eternity.

Yeshua was not diminishing the importance of the family, he was emphasizing it. How so? He was saying to his talmidim, 'When you are committed to doing the will of God, you are what a family is supposed to be. The members of a family should bless and serve one another. When you do that, then you will be my family — my mother, my brothers, and my sisters.'

In the New Covenant we have an extended family, the Kahal of the Lord. Abraham is called the father, not the production manager, of all those who believe. It is the family that provides the greatest example for the Kahal of human love. Our commitment to our earthly family is not severed; it is encompassed in our commitment to the Lord. We serve our family as the Lord commands us, which is not necessarily the same as doing whatever they say to do.

The family of Yeshua came to take "custody" of him — to get him away from his God-given responsibility. That he could not do, but he was not any the less committed to his family. Yeshua put forward the love and commitment of family members to one another as the model to imitate. We know that Yeshua's mother became a believer, as did his brothers Jacob, Judah, and Simeon. Even in the agony of the *tzelav*, he took care of his mother. (Jn.19:26-27)

The first talmid, Andrai, went and got his brother, Simon Kefa, to come follow Yeshua. The brothers Jacob and Yochanan became talmidim together. There is a relationship between the resurrection of Lazarus and the love that his sisters, Marta and Miryam, had for him.

Kefa said to Yeshua, "Behold, we have left everything and followed you." Yeshua said, "Truly I say to you, there is no one who has left house or brothers or sisters or mother or father or children or farms, for my sake and for the sake of the kingdom message, but that he shall receive a hundred times as much now in the present age, houses and brothers and sisters and mothers and children and farms, along with persecutions; and in the age to come, eternal life." (Mk.10:28-30)

Making your commitment to Yeshua may mean that your family will reject you, but you still must make that commitment. Since there is no higher commitment than that to the Lord, he promises to restore to you, along with eternal life, whatever you lose in making that commitment.

Part of that restoration is to take place in a local congregation, the most visible manifestation of the Kahal. The Messianic Writings do not say specifically that every believer has to be part of a local congregation; they simply assume it. The New Covenant is a corporate covenant.

When God wanted people sent forth to other lands with the message of the kingdom, He spoke to the elders in Antioch: "'Set apart for Me Barnabas and Shaul for the work to which I have called them.' Then, when they had fasted and prayed and laid their hands on them, they sent them away." (Acts 13:2-3)

The local congregation sent them out, they went and did the work, and then they came back and reported to the same congregation that had sent them out. They were accountable. One of the great blessings of a family is that they know you. You can fool people you meet, even people you see once a week, but your family knows what living with you is like. So even if your words are very smooth, your family still knows the real you, the good and the bad.

Commitment to a family often brings a few bruises with it, but that is part of life and growing up. On the other hand, being part of a family means that there are brothers and sisters who are committed to you. They will stand with you and help you. We don't usually choose the members of our family; but we do choose to affirm the choice that God has made.

A local congregation is much the same. There are people who will rub you the wrong way. They will grind you down, knock you over, and push you beyond what you can take. You might not like the way they do something, and they might not like the way you do something, but Yeshua is giving you the opportunity to deny yourself and become more like Him. We don't choose our earthly family, and they don't choose us. We learn to live with them, and we learn to change.

God places people where He wants them. He doesn't give us a choice, except to obey or disobey. God may place you with people whom you don't like and don't want to be with. When you find yourself with God-given responsibility — and every believer does — and God calls you to do something, you do it. It may not be easy, but you stick with it, and work it through.

Shaul wrote to the congregation in Rome (chapter 16): "Greet the congregation which meets in the house of ... Greet so and so and those set apart with them ..." The different congregations of a city are related to each other. As members of a larger family, they should be committed to one another and should work together.

Shaul came and submitted his teaching to Jacob and the elders in Yerushalayim, fearing that he might have laboured in vain. Shaul knew that God had instructed and sent him, but still he came and submitted to Jacob, the brethren, and the congregation in Yerushalayim. They recognized that God had appointed Shaul to reach the Gentiles, and gave him the right hand of fellowship. (Gal.2:9)

Years earlier, decrees from the congregation in Yerushalayim had gone out to all the congregations among the Gentiles instructing them about things they must not do. No one questioned its authority to do that. It was understood. The congregations among the Gentiles, hundreds of miles away, had never met these leaders, but they submitted to their authority. Such authority that God has designated in the congregation is to be recognized. It may be the "congregations in the city of someplace," or some kind of association of like-minded congregations. That relationship is part of your commitment to the Lord.

God's work of redemption in the world requires that we work together. When those of those of like faith work together, it often produces larger associations. Someone has to produce the instructional literature, but not everyone does. Someone has to have a training school, a magazine, or whatever, but not everyone does. The different members of a family can perform different functions for each other. It is not necessary, or possible, for every or any local congregation to duplicate all the work of the whole Kahal. The organizations themselves do not possess life; they are formed to serve life.

The Kahal, or any local congregation, is ultimately defined in the Bible as a community of believers. Yeshua is the head of the Kahal, which is to seek to be faithful to Him only. We are commanded: "Do not be unequally yoked with unbelievers," because unbelievers are serving other gods and seeking other goals. A congregation is part of the larger body of Messiah, with a God-given faith and purpose. That faith and purpose may be expressed in a variety of ways , but their essence is Biblically-defined service to God.

Inasmuch as we are all in the process of being changed, the Scriptures evidence a certain amount of variety. The analogy of the body of Messiah, composed of different members, demands it. Yet, there are some congregations whose structure, belief, teaching, and actions are sufficiently contrary to the Bible, that they are not congregations of the Lord. There may be some believers in such gatherings, but, at some point, that is not what a congregation is. Nor is the crowd in a subway car or at a football game with the same mixture of believers and unbelievers. A congregation is united and motivated by faith in the Redeemer.

Havah was formed out of the side of Adam. When Yeshua hung on the *tzelav*, his side was pierced and the blood poured out. It is that blood that brings forgiveness to those who believe. The Kahal, the bride of Messiah, was formed out of the side of Yeshua. The Kahal is of him. It is made from him — bone and flesh, structure and content.

When there are disputes within the congregation, there are proper Biblical ways for handling them. Such disputes are family matters, to be governed according to already approved and established procedures. It is not appropriate for families to "air their dirty linen in public." As we are concerned for the growth and well-being of the whole of God's kingdom, we will be better able to fulfill our own individual purposes in that kingdom.

1. <u>The Pentateuch and Haftorahs</u>, edited by J.H. Hertz, Soncino Press, London, 1956, P.54

# 9. Commitment to

# PURITY

"Then God said to Abraham, 'As for you, you must keep My covenant, you and your descendants after you for the generations to come. This is My covenant with you and your descendants after you, the covenant you are to keep: Every male among you shall be circumcised. You are to undergo circumcision, and it will be the sign of the covenant between Me and you.' " (Gen. 17:9-11)

Circumcision of the male sexual organ is the sign of the covenant that God made with Abraham. That is an unusual sign, and for Abraham, who was 99 at the time, it was painful and perhaps a little embarrassing. What did he think? How would you explain to his household, which included hundreds of adult men (cf. Gen.14:14), what God had commanded for them? There were probably hundreds of boys in his household, too. Can you picture Abraham explaining to his friends (cf. Gen.14:13) what God had commanded?

On that very day that God spoke to him, Abraham had all the males of his household circumcised. (Gen. 17:23) That very day. That is obedience.

Circumcision is a very unusual sign. What does it signify? It signifies the circumcision of the heart that God has always desired of Israel (cf. Dt. 10:16; 30:6), but it signifies something more specific as well.

It signifies that Abraham and his seed, i.e. those who are physically descended from him, are set apart to the Lord. Separation to the Lord, i.e. holiness, includes the sexual and procreative aspects of life. It includes much more, but it certainly includes these. The most private, most intimate aspects of life are open before the Lord. God is holy, and His people must be holy too.

In the beginning, all that God created was good. His creation of mankind in His own image and likeness, male and female, was very good. Yet even what is very good can be defiled by sin. That is the nature of sin. It takes what is good and defiles it, makes it unclean.

The created differences in gender were very good. The desire for sexual relations was very good. All of this was a beautiful way of enabling humans to be fruitful and multiply; a beautiful way of enabling humans to give each other pleasure within the protection of love and responsibility. All of it was given within God's purposes. Unfortunately, all of it was defiled and distorted by sin, by man's decision to reject God's image and likeness within himself and to seek to craft his own identity apart from God.

God called Abraham and his descendants to be different from everyone else, and thereby to be a blessing to everyone else. His calling for Israel is explicit in terms of being a light to the Gentiles. (cf.Is. 42:6; 60:1-3) Jewish people are to call all the hopeless, grasping, dying rebels of the earth back to the light and life of God. Gentiles who are adopted children of Abraham, grafted into Israel's olive tree through Messiah, also share in this calling to bring reconciliation. (2Co. 5:18-19) Such a calling can only be fulfilled in holiness, in cleanliness, in purity. Will you live in such a way that God can use you to bring His light to those around you?

God destroyed the tribes in the land of Canaan because of their sexual immorality and idolatry. Before He brought Israel into the land, He spoke of the immorality of those nations and commanded us, "Do not defile yourselves in any of these ways, because this is how the nations that I am going to drive out before you became defiled. Even the land was defiled; so I punished it for its sin, and the land vomited out its inhabitants." (Lev. 18:24-25)

Unfortunately, we did not obey. Even before we entered the land, we were seduced into immorality by Midian. The leaders of Midian hired Balaam to curse Israel. God would not let him do that, but Balaam counselled Midian to destroy Israel through sexual immorality. (Num. 22-25,31) Seduction coupled with lust brought a devastating plague. There were those who wept before the Lord over this degradation of Israel, but there were also those who flaunted their sin. (Num.25:6) All those who defiled themselves were destroyed.

During the time we lived in the land also, uncleanness and immorality spread. We made ourselves incapable of faithfully representing a pure and holy God. Though some were faithful, Israel as a whole was incapable of being a light to the Gentiles. God brought judgment again and again, but we would not let go of our immorality. So He exiled us from the land which we, as the tribes of Canaan before us, had defiled. He promised, "I will disperse you among the Gentiles and scatter you through the countries; and I will put an end to your uncleanness." (Ezek. 22:15)

Things did not change after the return from captivity. We still did not understand or accept God's purpose, which was so much higher than the standard we were willing to accept. We did not put marriage in its proper place - "they shall be one flesh." (Gen.2:24) Two bodies coming together physically, whether in marriage or outside of marriage, is not just a physical act. It has spiritual significance before God.

We were unfaithful, but could not understand why God did not honor our prayers, offerings, and tears. "You ask, 'Why?' It is because the LORD is acting as the witness between you and the wife of your youth, because you have broken faith with her, though she is your partner, the wife of your marriage covenant." (Mal. 2:14)

Whether you are married or not, whether you are physically descended from Abraham or not, God has called you to purity. As Shaul wrote, "This I say therefore, and testify in the Lord, that you no longer walk as the rest of the Gentiles also walk, in the futility of their mind, being darkened in their understanding, alienated from the life of God, because of the ignorance that is in them, because of the hardening of their hearts; who, having become callous, gave themselves up to licentiousness to crave to do everything unclean. But you did not learn Messiah that way." (Eph.4:17-20)

Living for Messiah requires that we be clean, holy, set apart to God. "Make every effort to live in peace with all men and to be holy; without holiness no one will see the Lord." (Heb. 12:14) The person who chooses what feels good over what is good, will not enter into God's kingdom. The mind of man can be very creative, especially with a little help from the Adversary, in rationalizing and justifying what God forbids.

The Adversary convinced Havah that God was lying to her. He convinced her that God was keeping her from enjoying life to the fullest. He convinced her that life was meant to be lived independently of God. Havah and her husband believed the Serpent's lies, and rejected God's Truth. They rebelled.

But God had created Adam and Havah. God had created the garden and everything in it. He had created the sun, the moon, and the stars. He had created everything. God had walked with Adam and Havah, and talked with them. He had loved them, and the light of His face had shined upon them.

But they chose to believe the Serpent. Who was he? What did they know about him? Not much, just enough to call him a serpent. What had he done for them. Nothing. Why did they believe him? It's impossible to understand. And yet, they believed the Serpent for exactly the same reasons that we and those around us are tempted to believe him. Their own lust blinded them.

"Let no man say when he is tempted, 'I am tempted by God,' for God cannot be tempted by evil, and He himself tempts no one. But each one is tempted when he is drawn away by his own lust, and enticed. Then the lust, when it has conceived, gives birth to sin; and the sin, when it is full grown, brings forth death. **Do not be deceived**, my beloved brethren." (Jacob 1:13-16)

The Scriptures remind us not be deceived by the lust of the flesh. "**Do not be deceived.** God is not mocked, for whatever a man sows, that will he also reap. For he who sows to his own flesh will from the flesh reap corruption. But he who sows to the Spirit will from the Spirit reap eternal life." (Gal.6:7-8)"Or do you not know that the unrighteous will not inherit the Kingdom of God? **Do not be deceived.**" (1Cor. 6:9)

"Know this for sure, that no sexually immoral person, nor unclean person, nor covetous man, who is an idolater, has any inheritance in the Kingdom of Messiah and God. **Let no one deceive you with empty words**, for because of these things, the wrath of God comes on the children of disobedience. Therefore do not be partakers with them." (Eph.5:6-7)

In a society and world that pours a flood of glamorized filth at us, how can we escape? **The first step is to make a decision in our hearts to desire and** choose the supernatural way, the way of holiness. "Above all else, guard your heart, for it is the wellspring of life." (Prov. 4:23) What is in your heart will come out in your life. If you choose holiness, God will strengthen you in that decision. The choice, however, is yours.

**The second step is to receive the grace of God to live in that decision.** God gives grace to the humble. (cf. Prov. 3:34; Jacob 4:6; 1Pet. 5:5) If we let pride guide us, we will fall short of the grace of God, i.e. we will fall. If we humble ourselves before Him, He will give us sufficient grace, no matter what the circumstances.

God's grace, however, only enables us to choose what is right. It doesn't force us to choose what is right. We can receive His grace or we can reject it. The choice remains ours. That is why we must first make sure our hearts are pointed in the right direction.

If our hearts are steadfastly pointed in the right direction, we will gladly receive His grace to walk in purity. If our hearts entertain, encourage, and embrace lust, we will not want His grace. It would be a fatal mistake to reject the grace that God gives to us. (cf. 2Co.6:1-2)

**The third step is to use our minds.** If we add fuel to a fire, it will burn hotter. If we do not add fuel, the fire will go out. This is true no matter what kind of fire it is. We can fuel our spiritual hunger and burn for God, or we can fuel our physical desires and burn with lust.

The process of addiction to alcohol has been explained this way: First, the man takes a drink. Then the drink takes a drink. Then, the drink takes the man. The same applies to other addictions. For the moment, it may be easy to give in, but it is not easy to get out.

You are responsible for yourself. God loves you, and wants you to walk in purity, but it is your responsibility. It is not your shepherd's responsibility. It is not your parents' or teachers' or friends' responsibility. It is your responsibility. Feed the fire of your love for God. Do not feed the fire of your lust.

In this world, that means making conscious decisions to turn away from whatever else is pushing against you; to be more interested in what is eternally real than what is momentarily seductive. It doesn't matter what everyone else is watching or doing. Everyone else, just as you and I, one by one, will give account to God.

Make godly decisions for yourself. Don't hide in the darkness, walk in the light. God has much better things prepared for those who love Him. "Since we have these promises, dear friends, let us purify ourselves from everything that contaminates body and spirit, perfecting holiness in the fear of God." (2Cor. 7:1)

We are called to be different. "We know that we are children of God, and that the whole world is under the control of the evil one. " (1Jn. 5:19) We can't always control the images, voices, and thoughts that are thrown at us, but we can choose what we receive and what we reject. We can choose our focus. We can choose to actively walk in a different direction, to actively pursue different goals.

You cannot argue with your fleshly desires. You cannot change them. You will never convince them. Do not let their selfish whinings monopolize your thoughts. "For the mind directed towards the flesh is death, but the mind directed towards the Spirit is life and peace." (Rom.8:6)

Let your mind be set apart to serve God only. You do not need to think about unclean things. You do not need to analyze or understand them. You need to move to a different location. "Finally, brethren, whatever things are true, whatever things are honorable, whatever things are just, whatever things are pure, whatever things are lovely, whatever things are of good report; if there is any virtue, and if there is any praise, think about these things." (Phil.4:8)

Natural sight and hearing are good, but they can get us in trouble. To be servants of the Lord, we need to learn not to see and not to hear some things. Taste and touch are gifts from God, but they can be defiled and defiling. Make sure you keep your hands off what does not belong to you, i.e. what God has not apportioned to you. Keep your thoughts and your speech off these things, too.

As Kefa said, "Therefore, prepare your minds for action..." (1Pet. 1:13) Be ready. Be alert. Be actively engaged, with your thoughts, in seeking the kingdom of God.

**The fourth step is to repent if you start going the wrong way.** Do not quit. This is a battle. God is not giving up on you. Don't give up on God. Yield to God, and believe that He is able. He is able, and you should believe Him. He will deliver you and change you if you will let Him; if you will trust Him. Faith is the only way to overcome. (cf. 1Jn. 5:4)

King David fell into uncleanness, because he chose to stay home rather than go out and fight. He was protected, he was blessed, he was bored. He disappointed God, and he hurt a lot of other people. When confronted with his sin, he was broken, and cried out to God in repentance. "Create in me a pure heart, O God, and renew a steadfast spirit within me." (Ps. 51:10)

David saw that he was lost. He had dug a pit, fallen in, and couldn't get out. He knew that he needed more than forgiveness. He also needed a pure heart. He could not cleanse his heart himself. He could not just start over as he was. He needed God to do a supernatural work.

God created the entire universe out of nothing. He is

creating us anew in His image and likeness. If you start going the wrong way, if you fall, turn to God and cry out to Him. God wants us to walk with Him in holiness and humility. He has the power. We make the choice.

Purity in mind and body involves much more than sexual attitudes and activities. It involves a new way of thinking of yourself and other people. In Ephesians 4:22-32, Shaul wrote of many of the necessary changes. Put away lying, bitterness, and anger. Don't take what isn't yours. Instead, give to those in need. And, "Do not let any unwholesome talk come out of your mouths, but only what is helpful for building others up according to their needs, that it may benefit those who listen. ... Be kind and compassionate to one another, forgiving each other, just as in Messiah God forgave you." (Eph. 5:29,32

These are positive things. We cannot just avoid the negative, we need to be doing what is positive. What can you and God do together with the time you have? Build your faith, build your family, build your neighbor, build the kingdom. Make it your desire to spend time with Him, to know Him better, to grow in Him, to serve Him and those around you.

It can be very difficult to walk in purity in this world, but we cannot walk with God in any other way. We give up what is harmful to us and to others, and we receive what is good and clean, part of God's original intention. We receive the grace and strength of an almighty, holy, holy, holy Creator, Redeemer and Judge.

We let God prepare us for His coming kingdom. In the Messianic age, holiness will not only be supernatural, it will be natural, too. "And a highway will be there; it will be called the Way of Holiness. The unclean will not journey on it; it will be for those who walk in that Way; wicked fools will not go about on it." (Is. 35:8)

# 10. Commitment to

# GIVING

There are many incidents in Abraham's life that show how he viewed material possessions. He freely gave to God. And he was not motivated by any desire to accumulate for himself.

Lot's herdsmen quarreled with Abraham's herdsmen because of the limited land for their flocks. So Abraham said to Lot, "Is not the whole land before you? Please separate from me; if to the left, then I will go to the right; or if to the right, then I will go to the left." (Gen.13:9) As Lot's uncle, Abraham could have first chosen the best land for himself, and left the remainder for Lot. But Abraham was not pursuing wealth or possessions, even what was rightfully his, but righteousness. Lot chose the most fertile land for himself.

"And the Lord said to Abram, after Lot had separated from him, 'Lift up your eyes and look from the place where you are, northward and southward and eastward and westward; for all the land which you see, I will give it to you and to your seed forever.'" (Gen.13:14-15) After Abraham had shown that he was not striving for possessions, God gave him the promise that it would all be his. Abraham's wealth, possessions, and provisions came from God.

Soon afterwards, Lot, who was then living in Sedom, was taken captive by an invading army. When Abraham heard of it, he went in pursuit and rescued Lot, all the other captives, and their possessions. "And Melchizedek king of Salem brought out bread and wine; now he was a Kohen of God Most High. And he blessed him and said, 'Blessed be Abram of God Most High, possessor of heaven and earth; and blessed be God Most High, who has delivered your enemies into your hand.' And he [Abram] gave him a tenth of all." (Gen.14:18-20)

Abraham recognized God as his sovereign, and gave God a tenth of all he had received. God is the owner of heaven and earth. Everything belongs to Him. In material things, as in everything else, God comes first.

The king of Sedom then came and said to Abram, "'Give the people to me and take the goods for yourself.' And Abram said to the king of Sedom, 'I have sworn to the Lord God Most High, possessor of heaven and earth, that I will not take a thread or a sandal thong or anything that is yours, lest you should say, *I have made Abram rich.*'" (Gen.14:21-23) Since God owns heaven and earth, Abraham did not need what the king of Sedom had.

In the akedah, the offering up of Isaac, we can see the totality of Abraham's commitment to give to God. All that Abraham had, both people and things, he had received from the Lord. It all still belonged to God, who retained the right to do what He chose with it. Abraham was just taking care of these things for Him. In obedience, Abraham offered back to God what was most precious to him, his son Isaac.

Throughout his life, Abraham demonstrated a willingness to give from his heart to God. He often built altars, and offered sacrifices to the Lord. He was graciously hospitable to those who passed his tent. On one occasion, his three guests turned out to be two angels and the Lord.

God has freely given to us all things — life, light, air, warmth, food, love, and everything else that is good. In freely offering Isaac, Abraham represents the giving nature of God the Father. "For God so loved the world that He gave His only begotten Son that whosoever believes in Him should not perish but have everlasting life." (Jn.3:16) God so loved that He gave. Salvation/ *yeshuah* is God's free gift to man, at great expense to Himself. Those who are truly children of Abraham and children of God, should so love that they give, too. Yeshua told His talmidim, "freely you received, freely give."(Mt.10:8)

God told Moses, "'Tell the sons of Israel to take an offering for Me; from every man whose heart moves him you shall take My offering.' ... And everyone whose heart stirred him and everyone whose spirit moved him came and brought the Lord's offering for the work of the tent of meeting and for all its service and for the holy garments ... and they said to Moses, 'The people are bringing much more than enough for the service for the work which the Lord commanded us to perform.'"(Ex.25:2; 35:21; 36:5)

Rabbi Hertz comments, "The construction of the Tabernacle thus became an external sign of love and gratitude and surrender to God's will."[1] Temples, palaces, and pyramids were usually built with slave labour, but the people of God are not forced to give. They choose to do so.

The people gave because their hearts moved them to give — to give to the Lord who had redeemed them, to build something for Him. We give because the Lord has done so much for us and given so much to us, and we are grateful. At Sinai, the people gave so freely that Moses had to command them to stop. They had the opportunity to give to God for His work, and they took full advantage of it. There was nothing better or more wonderful that they could do with what they had. Much of what they gave had come from their Egyptian neighbors on the night of redemption — God had moved the Egyptians to give.

Only God can create. Whatever material possessions or wealth you have belongs to Him. You might have worked for it, someone might have given it to you; but the world and all that it contains belong to God, the Creator. When we give to God our Redeemer, we are the ones who are enriched.

As the Lord said to Israel before He brought us into the land, "The land must not be sold permanently, because the land is Mine and you are but aliens and My tenants." (Lev. 25:23) What is true of the land of Israel is also true of all the people of Israel, "for the children of Israel belong to Me as servants. They are My servants, whom I brought out of Egypt. I am the LORD your God." (Lev. 25:55) We, and all we have, belong to Him. Therefore, we are actively concerned about the welfare of our brethren.

Shaul wrote to the believers at Corinth, "Brethren, we wish to make known to you the grace of God which has been given in the congregations of Macedonia, that in a great ordeal of affliction, their abundance of joy and their deep poverty overflowed in the wealth of their liberality; for I testify that according to their ability — and BEYOND their ability — they gave of their own accord, begging us with much entreaty for the favor of participation for the support of those set apart, and this, not as we had expected, but they first gave themselves to the Lord and to us by the will of God." (2 Cor.8:1-5)

The Macedonian believers were afflicted and poor, but they gave more than what they were able to give; and they did it willingly and with an abundance of joy. Their deep poverty highlighted the wealth of their giving. They begged for the privilege of participating in the support of those set apart, i.e., the Jewish believers in Yerushalayim. After having given generously to advance the work of the Lord, these Jewish believers were having difficulty because of a famine. The Macedonian believers gave themselves wholly, first to God, and then to His servants.

People give themselves to causes, to other people, to consuming desires. Their lives are fragmented as they are torn one way and then another by what they have given themselves to serve. "Do you not know that to whom you yield yourselves as bondservants to obedience, to him whom you obey you are bondservants; whether of sin unto death, or of obedience unto righteousness?"(Rom.6:16)

In giving ourselves wholly to the Lord, we give our time, our talent, and our resources. We may not control whether we have abundance or poverty, whether we are afflicted or exalted, but we choose our master — the one to whom our hearts belong. Everyone, whether pauper or king, is on the same ground. What matters is not what you have, but what you choose. We understand that choosing to serve God means choosing to serve people made in His image and likeness. We cannot love God without loving our neighbor.

Time is the measure of the quantity of our lives. It is the means by which we show who is Lord in our lives. That is why we are commanded, "Whatsoever you do, do it unto the Lord, and not unto men." (Col.3:23) If you do what you do in service to Yeshua, then he will reward you. It is better to give whatever talents and abilities you have to God for the spread of His Kingdom than to squander them on yourself, give them to a friend, or hide them in the ground. No one is called to be a spectator in the kingdom of God; everyone is called to be a citizen and laborer.

Concerning whatever of the Lord's money He has entrusted to you, God says: "'Bring the whole tithe into the storehouse, so that there may be food in My house; and test Me now in this,' says the Lord of Hosts, 'if I will not open for you the windows of heaven and pour out for you a blessing until it overflows. Then I will rebuke the devourer for you ...'" (Mal.3:10,11)

A tithe is a tenth. The Lord's tithe is the first tenth of whatever wealth you gain. That first tenth comes before the government has taken what it wants, before the loan company takes what it wants, and before everything and anything else. The tithes supported the kohanim and Levites, the ministers of God. It was their means of living. If the people didn't tithe, the Levites and the kohanim had to leave the Temple to go find some other means of providing for themselves and their families. When the people do not tithe, those to whom the Lord has given positions of responsibility cannot serve before the Lord. The tithe of His people is the Lord's method for sustaining those to whom He has given positions of responsibility.

Hundreds of years before the Lord instituted the covenant of the Law at Mt. Sinai, Abraham tithed. Jacob also tithed. (Gen.28:22) Tithing is the way of the children of Abraham. The obligation to tithe does not come from Sinai or from the Rabbis. It comes from God's ownership of all creation.

In rebuking the scribes and Pharisees for their hypocrisy, Yeshua said, "You hypocrites, you tithe your garden herbs, but you neglect the weightier matters of the Law; justice, mercy, and faith. These are the things you should have done without neglecting the others."(Mt.23:23) Yeshua did not say, 'Do not tithe!' He was telling them, 'You should tithe, but don't think that giving money is a substitute for doing justice, or showing mercy and faith.'

Shaul told Timothy to instruct the congregation, "Let

the elders who rule well be considered worthy of double honor, especially those who work hard at teaching and proclaiming, for the Scripture says, 'You shall not muzzle the ox while he is threshing,' and 'the labourer is worthy of his wages.'" (1Tim.5:17,18) The word used here for "honor" is the one from which we derive "honorarium." Shaul is saying, 'Give them double pay. The laborer should be paid for his work, so bring in your tithes and offerings so that the elders may receive the sustenance that God has ordained for them; so that they may serve as God has called them.'

God also requires that we bring offerings to serve and worship Him. In tithing and giving offerings, the children of Abraham demonstrate: 1) Obedience, since God has commanded it; 2) Faith, since they believe that God will provide; 3) Hope, since they are living for God's kingdom rather than the kingdoms of the here and now; 4) Love, since they care whether or not others hear the kingdom message; and 5) Gratitude, since they want to express their thanks for what God has done.

The one who will not tithe is willfully demonstrating a lack of obedience, faith, hope, love, and gratitude. These things are the fruit of the Spirit in our lives. How then could such a person be rightly committed to the Lordship of Yeshua? Good fruit characteristically flows from the life of a believer.

Zakkai was a tax collector, a publican, the most despised of men, but he went to see Yeshua. Yeshua looked at him and said, "Zakkai, today I must eat at your house." And Zakkai said, "'Behold, Lord, half of my possessions I will give to the poor, and if I have taken anything from anyone unjustly, I will repay it fourfold.' And Yeshua said to him, 'Today salvation has come to this house, because he, too, is a son of Abraham.'" (Lk.19:8,9)

Why did Yeshua say that salvation had come to Zakkai and his household, and that Zakkai really was a son of Abraham? Simply because Zakkai gave — i.e., he repented and made restitution. He was not saved by giving, but the giving was a demonstration that Mammon was no longer Lord of his life; God was.

Throughout the Scriptures, God shows great concern for the poor. He commands us to show such concern as well. "He who is kind to the poor lends to the LORD, and He will reward him for what he has done." (Prov. 19:17) Zakkai demonstrated his change of heart.

Something else should be noted about the giving of finances. Shaul encouraged the Gentile belivers in Rome to send a relief offering to the believers in Yerushalayim. "But now I am going to Yerushalayim, serving those set apart; for Macedonia and Achaia have been pleased to make a contribution for the poor among those set apart in Yerushalayim. Yes, they were pleased to do so, and they are indebted to them; for if the Gentiles have shared in their spiritual things, they are indebted to minister to them also in material things." (Ro.15:25-27) Gentile Believers owe a debt to the Jewish people for the kingdom message and for all the things of God - a debt they truly cannot repay. Nevertheless, in gratitude, they are to give material things in return.

Yeshua was in the Temple, by the treasury, when an elderly widow came, after the "big spenders" had dropped in their large sums . She dropped in two small copper coins. "And calling his talmidim to him, he said to them, "Truly I say to you, this poor widow put in more than all those who were putting in to the treasury; for they all put in out of their abundance, but she, out of her poverty, put in all she owned, all she had to live on." (Mk.12:43-44)

What kind of accounting system does God use? He

doesn't count how much you give, but rather how much you have left over. The poor widow didn't have any left over; that's why her gift was greater than all the rest put together. They gave out of their abundance, with plenty left over. She didn't even have left what she needed.

The Macedonian believers gave willingly so that "their deep poverty overflowed in the wealth of their liberality." So did this poor widow. It is not how much you give compared to someone else that is important. It is the total giving of yourself and all that you have, as Abraham did, that God is looking for.

1. <u>The Pentateuch and Haftorahs</u>, edited by J.H. Hertz, Soncino Press, London, 1956, P.326

# 11. Commitment to

# AUTHORITY

When the Lord told Abraham to leave everything behind to follow Him, Abraham obeyed. When He told Abraham to offer up Isaac, Abraham did not question God's absolute right to command and to be obeyed. Abraham did not challenge God's right to come first before his own human desires and reasonings, and before the customs and laws of men. When God instituted circumcision as the sign of the covenant, and when He promised to supernaturally enable Sarah to conceive Isaac, Abraham did not question God's right to order the most intimate affairs of his life, or to overrule the laws of nature.

When God promised to give Abraham all the land he could see, and when God promised to bless those who blessed Abraham and curse those who cursed him, Abraham did not doubt God's authority to rule over and judge His creation. God's authority was never an issue in Abraham's life, because Abraham recognized that God has the right, the jurisdiction, and the power to be obeyed in everything.

Shaul told the believers in Rome, "Let every soul be in subjection to the authorities above, for there is no authority except from God, and those which exist have been set in order by God. Therefore he who sets himself against the authority, resists the ordinance of God; and those who resist will receive judgment to themselves." (Rom.13:1,2)

God is the one who authorizes whatever is authorized, because He is the only authority there is. He is Lord of all. All are required to obey Him. All the authorities which He has established exist simply to serve Him. When we commit ourselves to obey God's authority, we commit ourselves to obey, as our father Abraham did, the authorities which God has established. Failure to do so would be to oppose the ordinance of God, and to insure His condemnation. When a man rebels against his king, he can expect to face consequences.

When David was in hiding from King Saul, he and his men protected the flocks of Nabal in the wilderness. When Nabal was shearing his sheep and rejoicing in his prosperity, David sent men to request of him that he share some of his bounty with them. "But Nabal answered David's servants, and said, 'Who is David? And who is the son of Jesse? There are many servants today who are each breaking away from his master.'" (1 Sam.25:10)

Certainly Nabal had a point: there are many who claim to be somebody or to have some authority, but it is only their own imagination and pride. God, the author of authority, has not authorized them. Unfortunately for Nabal, David was not such a pretender. David was the Lord's anointed, and he and his men had protected Nabal's flocks. In rejecting David, Nabal was rejecting the Lord. Resisting proper authority is the same as resisting God.

There are some who have been authorized by God for one thing, but claim authority in another, or in everything. They are in rebellion against the authority of God, and to yield to their rebellion would be to join it. If God has not given the authority, then no authority exists.

The Kohen HaGadol and the Council commanded the talmidim to stop proclaiming in the name of Yeshua. "But Kefa and the ambassadors answered and said, 'We must obey God rather than men.'" (Acts 5:29) God had authorized the proclaiming of the kingdom message. He did not give anyone authority to stop those who were proclaiming that message. The Council had no authority for making such a command. That is why the believers did not obey the command then, or ever. Sometimes that meant being physically beaten. Sometimes it meant being imprisoned. Sometimes, being murdered. Whatever the cost, they have chosen to be faithful to the Lord, and to His authority.

In the centuries since, countless other believers have also chosen to refuse to obey such unlawful decrees. They have rejected the commands of those who falsely claimed to exercise God's authority, those who forbid what God not only permitted but commanded.

On the other hand, there are those who have been given proper authority by God, but fail to exercise it. Submission to God's authority is a two-edged sword; we must obey those over us, and we must command those under us. Failure to do either is a failure to submit to the authority that God has established.

A centurion whose servant needed to be healed came to Yeshua and said, "'Lord, I am not worthy for You to come under my roof, but just say the word and my servant will be healed. For I, too, am a man under authority, with soldiers under me; and I say to this one, "Go!" and he goes, and to another, "Come!" and he comes, and to my slave, "Do this!" and he does it.' Now when Yeshua heard, He marveled, and said to those who were following, 'Truly I say to you, I have not found such great faith not even in Israel.'" (Mt.8:8-10)

The centurion did not say, "I am a man WITH

authority, but rather, "I am a man UNDER authority." He was under the authority of the Imperial government of Rome. When he spoke, those soldiers moved, not because of him, but because all the power of the Roman Empire was behind him. Anyone, other than God, who is to properly exercise authority over others must be UNDER authority.

Yeshua indicated that the kind of faith we should have recognizes this; it recognizes God's authority. If God says the word, it will be done. To recognize and be properly committed and submitted to God's authority, we must know what authorities God has established. There are several major ones that affect our lives continually.

The first is **PERSONAL AUTHORITY**, recognized in two ways: 1) God's authority in making you. Don't be as a pot saying to the Potter, "Why did you make me like this? and not like some other pot?" The pot should recognize that the Potter knows what He's doing. Recognize His authority to make you for His purposes and to do in your life whatever He chooses to do. Accept His discipline and purpose in your life. Kefa said, 'What about Yochanan?' And Yeshua answered, 'That is not your business. You are to keep your eyes on me.' (cf. Jn.21:20-24)

Recognizing God's authority in this way will keep you free from jealousy. Jealousy destroys those it captures, and keeps them from realizing who they actually are. God did not shortchange anyone in making us. He made each one according to His plan, for His reasons. He has something for each one to do in His kingdom, something to do in this world to glorify Him. No matter what He has given to anyone else, be submitted to God's authority in making you; for it is through the lives of its different members that the body of the Lord is wholly revealed; in sorrow and joy, glory and shame, strength and weakness.

2) Personal authority is also recognized in God's authority, entrusted to you, over your own decisions. You are responsible for the decisions you make. You are to be the manager, although not the owner, of your own life. No matter what mistakes your parents made, no matter what some teacher said to you in the third grade, you, and no one else, are responsible for the decisions that you make, and their consequences. If you choose to let someone else decide for you, that is your decision, for which you will give account. We need to accept responsibility and learn to do what is right, without looking for scapegoats.

The second kind of authority that God has established is **FAMILY AUTHORITY,** given to husbands and to parents. The husband is ultimately responsible, by God's design, for the decisions of the family. He will give account to God for how he has exercised that authority, in harshness or in gentleness, in selfishness or in service.

"Husbands, love your wives, just as Messiah also loved the Kahal and gave himself up for it; that he might sancify it, having cleansed it by the washing of water with the word." (Eph.5:25-26) The husband is to exercise the Lord's authority, as Messiah did, in servanthood. Yeshua gave everything, even his life, for the benefit of those who, though then his enemies, would repent and be joined together as his bride.

Given that, "Wives, be subject to your own husbands, as to the Lord. For the husband is the head of the wife, as Messiah also is the head of the Kahal, he himself being the savior of the body." (Eph.5:22-23) To submit to man because we are submitted to God requires great faith.

A wife is to submit to her husband as she would submit to the Lord, although he is not the Lord. For that she will give account to God, because it is He who has entrusted the authority to her husband. The husband will give account for how he exercises that authority.

God has also established parental authority over children. "Children, obey your parents in the Lord. This is well-pleasing to the Lord, and it has a good promise for you, 'that it may be well with you and your days may be long upon the land which the Lord God gives you.' And fathers, do not provoke your children to anger; but bring them up in the discipline and instruction of the Lord." (Eph.6:1-4) Parents exercise the authority of the Lord in the nurture and training of their children. The parents must exercise it as the Lord would, and the children must obey it as though it were done by the Lord.

The family is the training ground for parents, that they might be given authority in the congregation; and for children, that they might be trained to obey the voice of the Lord. How well they will be able to obey the voice of the Lord is in great measure determined by how they respond to their parents. This is the first encounter with God's authority that a child has. This is where children come to grips with the kingdom of God, obeying God's authority in their parents. This is also where **parents** come to grips with the kingdom of God, learning to serve God by training their children.

**SOCIETAL AUTHORITY** is multifaceted, but the Bible deals explicitly with the employer-employee relationship. "Servants, obey those who are your physical masters, with fear and trembling, in the sincerity of your heart, as to Messiah; not by way of eyeservice, as men-pleasers, but as slaves of Messiah, doing the will of God from the heart. With good will render service, as to the Lord, and not to men, knowing that whatever good thing each one does, this he will receive back from the Lord, whether slave or free. You masters, do the same things to them, and refrain from threatening, knowing that He who is both their Master and yours is in heaven, and there is no judging by outward appearance with Him." (Eph.6:5-9)

God entrusts His authority to masters to be exercised as He Himself would exercise it, and, consequently, He expects servants to obey their masters as they would Him. Most of us do not live in societies which still have slavery or indentured servitude. For that, we should be grateful, and we should seek the freedom of those who do not yet enjoy it. The principle, however, still applies to employer- employee relationships. No matter what our status or position in this world, we will all give account to God. To serve God well we must serve well those over us, and those under us.

In a similar way, God's authority is entrusted to other kinds of organizations and structures in society, for there is no authority except that which is of God. It is not the employer's or the chairman's authority. It is God's authority. Those who exercise it will give account for how they exercise.it Those under it will give account for how they obey it.

God has established **CONGREGATIONAL AUTHORITY** — that of ambassadors, shepherds, teachers, and others in the congregation. In Hebrews 13 we are told, "Remember those who led you, who spoke the word of God to you, and, considering the result of their conduct, imitate their faith ... Obey your leaders and submit to them. They keep watch over your souls as those who will give an account. Let them do this with joy and not with grief, for this would be unprofitable for you." (vv.7,17)

The congregational leaders must give account to God for how they exercise the authority that God lays out for them in His word. They are to watch over the souls of those who are to submit to that authority. It is an authority which is given to shepherd, to train, to make talmidim. It is not an authorisation to run people's lives and make their decisions for them. That authority has already been given to the individual.

In his messages to the seven congregations (Revelation 2 & 3) Yeshua often reminds the individual congregations to take responsibility for doctrine and internal discipline. Failure to do so will cause great problems, and will bring the chastening discipline and judgment of God.

God has given **STATE AUTHORITY** to bear the sword, internally and externally — to punish evildoers, and to protect the righteous. To accomplish this, God has given the State authority to levy taxes as defined in His Word, but not to enslave the people by stealing from them. Every authority that God establishes is defined in His Word. In this area, as in all, there is a difference between what men command and what God has authorized. Power that comes against the authorities God has established is to be resisted. "Can a corrupt throne be allied with you — one that brings on misery by its decrees?" (Ps. 94:20) Legitimate authority, however, even if it causes great inconvenience, is to be obeyed.

In a sermon entitled, "The Source and Bounds of Kingly Power," John Knox pointed out that, "Kings, then, have not an absolute power to do in their government what pleases them but their power is limited by God's Word; so that if they strike where God has not commanded, they are but murderers; and if they spare where God has commanded to strike, they and their throne are criminal and guilty of the wickedness which abounds upon the face of the earth, for lack of punishment."[1]

God has also entrusted a certain measure of His authority to every believer — the **AUTHORITY OF THE BELIEVER** — in the physical and spiritual realm. Yeshua said, "I cast out demons with the finger of God." (Lk. 11:20) It was not by physical power, but by the authority of God. When he sent out the twelve talmidim, he gave them that same power and authority to cast out demons, to heal diseases, and to raise the dead. (Mt.10:1)

They did not know how to do these things. All they knew was that they had been given the authority. So just as a policeman directs the traffic flow of numerous vehicles that could easily, any one of them, crush him to death, the talmidim began to use that authority. They were amazed to see that it worked. They said to the diseases, "Be gone!" to the people, "Be healed!" to the demons, "I cast you out!" and it happened.

Yeshua told his talmidim, "Behold I have given you authority to tread upon serpents and scorpions, and over all the power of the enemy, and nothing shall injure you; nevertheless, do not rejoice in this, that the spirits are subject to you, but rejoice that your names are recorded in heaven." (Lk.10:19,20) Even as we witness God's miraculous power, we are to remember the longing of God's heart that men repent, believe, and become talmidim of the Kingdom of God.

In the midst of a violent, life-threatening storm, Yeshua was awakened by the talmidim, who thought they would perish. "He stood up, and he rebuked the wind and the sea, and they were calm." (Lk. 8:24) Yeshua exercised authority over creation. He multiplied loaves and fishes, and commanded the forces of nature. He still has that authority, and exercises it.

Yehoshua told the sun and the moon to stand still,

and they obeyed, because he spoke with the authority of God. He couldn't explain to the sun and the moon how to stand still, he just told them to do it. Then, the supernatural God who created the natural world caused His creation to obey.

Yeshua also exercised, and entrusted to his talmidim, the authority to bind and loose. In the rabbinic sense, the authority to bind and to loose was the authority to say, "THIS is prohibited, and THAT is allowed." Yeshua told the talmidim, "Truly I say to you, whatever you shall bind on earth shall be bound in heaven; and whatever you loose on earth shall be loosed in heaven." (Mt.18:18) That is a great responsibility, legitimate only in the sphere of authority entrusted to them.

Yeshua also demonstrated both his authority to heal and his authority to forgive sin. "And behold, they were bringing to him a paralysed man lying on a bed; and Yeshua seeing their faith said to the paralytic, 'Take courage, my son, your sins are forgiven.' And behold, some of the scribes said to themselves, 'This fellow blasphemes.' And Yeshua, knowing their thoughts, said, 'Why are you thinking evil in your hearts? For which is easier, to say, 'Your sins are forgiven.' or to say, 'Rise and walk'? But in order that you may know that the Son of Adam has authority on earth to forgive sin' — Then he said to the paralyzed man, 'Rise, take up your mat and go home.' And he rose, and went home." (Mt.9:2-7)

The Lord delegates his authority as he chooses. After Yeshua had been raised from the dead, he appeared to the talmidim, who were fearfully hiding, "and said to them, 'Receive the Ruakh HaKodesh. If you forgive the sins of any, their sins have been forgiven them; if you retain the sins of any, they have been retained.'" (Jn.20:22-23) We should recognize and practice this authority to forgive those who sin against us.

Yeshua himself demonstrated other authority which is relevant to every believer. God commanded Israel to rest and not work on Shabbat, the seventh day. Sometimes, Yeshua healed people on Shabbat, which angered those who thought that healing was work which profaned Shabbat. But one must know the will of the Father in order to do the will of the Father.

God made a covenant with Israel, and gave Shabbat as a sign of it. (Ex.31:12-17) He defined the covenant, and knows His own purposes, His "original intent." Yeshua told us that, "Shabbat was made for the sake of Adam, and not Adam for the sake of Shabbat. Consequently, the Son of Adam is Lord even of Shabbat." (Mk.2:27-28)

God's purpose was that men should recognize their dependence on Him for all things; that they should acknowledge their inadequacy without Him. He did not want us to think that our own hard work, which He encourages, is sufficient to give us life. We must rest and trust in Him. Shabbat is not a ball and chain; it is a covenant sign, indicating the faith relationship that Israel is to have with her God. "For the one who has entered His rest has himself also rested from his works, as God did from His." (Heb.4:10)

Similarly, God's Holy Temple was never intended simply as a place of sacrifice and religious activity, but as a house of prayer for all the peoples. (Is.56:7) Yeshua cast the merchants and moneychangers out of the Temple, and the next day, "When he had come into the Temple, the chief Kohanim and the Elders of the people came to him as he was teaching, and said, 'By what authority are you doing these things, and who gave you this authority?' And Yeshua answered and said to them, 'I will ask you one thing too, which if you tell me, I will also tell you by what authority I do these things. The immersion/*tevilah* of Yochanan was from what source, from heaven or from men?'" (Mt.21:23-25)

Did God authorize this *tevilah*, or was it just a good idea that Yochanan had? They feared the multitude, but were unwilling to accept the truth, so they said, "We do not know." Inasmuch as they refused to recognize or submit to the authority of God in calling Israel to repentance through Yochanan, there was no point in telling them the source of Yeshua's authority. They understood clearly the importance of their question, but were unwilling to accept the answer. Yeshua was not, in any way, authorized by man, but, in every way, by the Father.

Likewise, "just as the Father has life in Himself, even so He gave to the Son also to have life in himself; and He gave him authority to execute judgment, because he is the Son of Adam." (Jn.5:26-27) He brings judgment, both temporal and eternal, on individuals and nations, because he has the authority to do so. We want men to repent that they might escape the judgment of God, but we are warned that most will not. Abraham interceded for Sedom and Amorrah, but he did not challenge God's authority to judge and destroy the wicked.

Occasionally believers are called to pronounce God's judgment. Kefa did. (Acts 5:1-11) Shaul did. (Acts 13:5-12) The prophets did. Some day, you may be called to do the same. Do not mistake that for a license to condemn and belittle others. "The wisdom that comes from above is first of all pure; then peace-loving, considerate, submissive, full of mercy and good fruit, impartial and without hypocrisy." (Jacob 3:17)

God is seeking "to bring many sons to glory," to raise up true children of Abraham who will faithfully exercise His authority and demonstrate His love. That is what

Yeshua summed up in calling his talmidim to fulfill the Great Commission: "And Yeshua came up and spoke to them, saying, 'All authority has been given to me in heaven and on earth. Go, therefore, and make talmidim of all the Gentiles, immersing them in the name of the Father, Son, and Ruakh HaKodesh, teaching them to observe all that I commanded you; and lo, I am with you all the days, even to the end of the age." (Mt.28:18-20) His talmidim have not been given free rein, but they have been entrusted with sufficient authority to do their job.

1. <u>Masterpieces of Pulpit Eloquence</u>, comp. Henry C. Fish, Vol. 1, Pt.2, F.M. Barton, Cleveland, 1907

# 12. Commitment to RIGHTEOUSNESS

The LORD appeared to Isaac and said, "Do not go down to Egypt; live in the land where I tell you to live. Stay in this land for a while, and I will be with you and will bless you. For to you and your descendants I will give all these lands and will establish the oath I swore to your father Abraham. I will make your descendants as numerous as the stars of the heavens and will give them all these lands, and through your offspring all nations on earth will be blessed, because Abraham listened to My voice and kept My charge, My commandments, My statutes and My laws." (Gen. 26:2-5)

God chose Abraham, and Abraham chose God. To choose God means to be faithful to the One who is the standard of right and wrong. It means to trust and obey Him. That is what Abraham did.

God told Isaac that Abraham

1. listened to My voice;
2. kept My charge;
3. kept My commandments, My statutes, and My laws.

**1. Abraham listened to God's voice.** This is a comprehensive expression of trust and obedience. It includes all the specifics that follow.

God's word is life. That is why the greatest commandment begins, "Hear, O Israel ..." As children of Abraham, we must listen to the voice of the Lord.

Before Israel entered the land, Moses summed up the

lesson of forty years in the wilderness. "He humbled you, causing you to hunger and then feeding you with manna, which neither you nor your fathers had known, to teach you that man does not live on bread alone but on every word that comes from the mouth of the LORD." (Deut. 8:3)

There are many voices in the world; many which claim to show the right way; many which claim they must be obeyed. To distinguish God's voice, we need a willing heart, i.e., whatever He says to us we will do, whether we want to or not. We will accept His "analysis" of what is right and what is wrong.

**2. Abraham kept God's charge/מִשְׁמַרְתִּי.** That means he watched over and took good care of what God had entrusted to him. He was faithful to his responsibility.

When God told Abram to leave his people and native land, he was faithful to do that. In the land to which God brought him, he was faithful to train his household in the way of the Lord. When God established circumcision as the sign of His covenant, Abraham was faithful to keep it.

Circumcision was a commandment, but it was also a charge, a responsibility. It signified that Abraham and all his descendants were set apart to God, called to be a separate, distinct people.

God's plan for redeeming mankind is integrally connected to that distinction. Israel does not exist for its own sake alone. God created the Jewish people as the means of bringing the Gentiles back to Himself. He called Israel to be a holy people who would represent Him to the world, and lead the world out of the darkness of unrighteousness into the light of righteousness. (Is. 43:10)

He established a covenant relationship with Israel, calling Himself the God of Israel. In that covenant relationship, He gave great promises of both blessing for faithfulness and judgment for disobedience. He caused His glory to dwell visibly in the midst of Israel, and revealed Himself as Father, Shepherd, Savior, Lord, and King.

Through the Jewish people, He has given to the world the Scriptures from Genesis to Revelation, including His holy Law. He has given the patriarchs, the prophets, and the Messiah. Through His New Covenant with Israel, all people can be brought to repentance, faith, and righteousness. And in the establishment of the kingdom of God on earth, which is God's ultimate purpose in creating the earth, the land of Israel will be the center, and Jerusalem will be the capital, of Messiah's kingdom.

Being Jewish is a responsibility that can only be fulfilled through a living relationship with the God who created the Jewish people. It is a responsibility that can only be fulfilled through receiving and giving His light. It is a responsibility that most shun because it is not usually easy or well appreciated, as all the prophets can attest. In a world that is trapped in darkness, hostile towards God, it is nevertheless the most essential of callings.

### 3. Abraham kept God's commandments/מצותי, statutes/חקותי, and laws/תורתי.

What commandments, decrees, and laws did Abraham keep? To answer that, we need to first look at what "law" means in the Bible.

God said, "Abraham kept "toratai/תורתי". The Hebrew word *torah* is usually translated as "law." It comes from a root that means "to flow." From that root meaning, it acquires the meaning "to give direction," or "to teach." The English word "law" is not really the equivalent of torah. "Teaching" might be a better word, but it does not convey the mandatory nature of what God teaches. Obeying God's teaching is not optional.

The Greek word "*nomos*/νομος" is used in the Septuagint and in the Messianic Writings to translate torah. *Nomos* also is usually translated as "law." It comes from a root that relates to prescribed usage, especially of pastureland. *Nomos* is not the exact equivalent of *torah*, but it faithfully indicates "what is permitted and what is prohibited." It faithfully indicates what the central issue is — how man should live.

In searching for the right English words to represent this reality, we are not far off in saying, "the law of God." We are talking about the divine order which God has established.

The law of God does not originate at Sinai. The law of God originates in God. The distinctions between right and wrong, good and evil, permitted and prohibited come from who God is. God has established an order in creation for all of His creatures.

God created Adam. That is why Adam should have trusted and obeyed God. It was the one and only thing that Adam needed to do. All that his descendants need to do is the same.

Adam and his descendants were created in the image and likeness of God. That is why it was wrong for Cain to kill Abel, even though "Thou shalt not murder" had not yet been engraved in stone. That is why, after the flood, God prescribed death for murderers. "Whoever sheds the blood of man, by man shall his blood be shed; because in the image of God has God made man.'" (Gen. 9:6) The prohibition against murder comes from the created nature of man in the image of God.

In the beginning, God made them male and female. "For this reason a man will leave his father and mother and be united to his wife, and they will become one flesh." (Gen. 2:24) That is why it was wrong for Abimelech — who was not Jewish, and who lived long before Moses was born — to take another man's wife. (cf. Gen.20:3-7) The prohibition against adultery comes from the created nature of man and woman in the image of God.

These and other such laws of God were given to all the descendants of Adam, long before Sinai, and long after it. Abraham walked in obedience to the law and teaching which God had placed within him.

In the Law of Moses, God includes all of His universal law for all mankind. These laws apply to Gentiles as well as to Jews. He also includes special laws and statutes to enable the people of Israel to fulfill the special purposes for which they were created. Inasmuch as God created Israel, that alone is sufficient reason for Israel to trust and obey Him.

There are specific laws that set Israel apart from the Gentiles as a holy people. That separation enabled God to enter into covenant relationship, communicate the Scriptures, teach the necessity of faith, and bring Messiah into the world.

There are also specific covenant signs that illustrate what God requires. These include circumcision, observing Shabbat, wearing tzitzit and tefillin, affixing a mezuzah to the doorpost, and not eating unclean animals. The feasts of the Lord (Lev.23) commemorate and illustrate different aspects of redemption. So do the commanded sacrifices and offerings.

All of these commandments, statutes, laws, and responsibilities are included in the greatest commandment of all: "Hear, O Israel: The LORD our God, the LORD is one. You shall love the LORD your God with all your heart and with all your soul and with all your strength." (Dt. 6:4-5) And because Adam was made in the image and likeness of God, there is another commandment that is similar to the greatest: "Love your neighbor as yourself." (Lev. 19:18)

All the rest of the Law of Moses gives concrete detail to these two great commandments. It is God's gracious gift to guide Israel in righteousness, to illustrate God's holiness to the Gentiles.

## The New Covenant and the Law

There is no problem with the Law God gave Israel at Sinai. The problem is with the lawbreakers. God's justice requires that the lawbreakers receive the penalty for breaking God's law.

"We all, like sheep, have gone astray, each of us has turned to his own way; and the LORD has laid on him the iniquity of us all." (Is. 53:6) Yeshua died to atone for our sin, not to make sin permissable. Sin is breaking God's law. (cf.1Jn.3:4) The solution to the problem of sin is not to get rid of the law, for it is holy, righteous, and good. That would create a lawless society. The solution is to transform the lawbreakers by changing their hearts.

God in His mercy has presented to Israel the New Covenant in Yeshua. He promised, " 'This is the covenant I will make with the house of Israel after that time,' declares the LORD. 'I will put My law in their minds and write it on their hearts.' " (Jer. 31:33)

That is why, in the New Covenant, God provides a way for us to walk in His holy, righteous, and good law. "And I will put My Spirit within you and cause you to walk in My decrees/חקותי, and you will keep and do My ordinances/משפטי." (Ezek. 36:27)

Yeshua suffered the penalty our iniquity deserves. In him we have the required offering for our guilt. "Yet it was the LORD's will to crush him and cause him to suffer, and though the LORD makes his life a guilt offering, he will see his offspring and prolong his days, and the will of the LORD will prosper in his hand." (Is. 53:10)

In him we die, that we might live. "For we know that our old self was crucified with him so that the body of sin might be done away with, that we should no longer be slaves to sin — because anyone who has died has been freed from sin.

"Do not offer the parts of your body to sin, as instruments of wickedness, but rather offer yourselves to God, as those who have been brought from death to life; and offer the parts of your body to him as instruments of righteousness." (Rom. 6:6,7,13)

"For the Law was powerless, in that it was weak through the flesh. God, sending his own Son in the likeness of sinful flesh and for sin, condemned sin in the flesh; that the righteous requirement of the Law might be fulfilled in us, who do not walk according to the flesh, but according to the Spirit." (Rom. 8:3-4)

### Abraham and God's Law

So what commandments, statutes, and laws of God did Abraham keep? The Law of Moses? No. That had not yet been given, and would not be given for another 400 years.

Abraham's marriage to Sarah shows clearly that God was not referring to the Law of Moses in His commendation of Abraham. In the Law of Moses, God commands, "Do not have sexual relations with your sister, either your father's daughter or your mother's daughter, whether she was born in the same home or elsewhere." (Lev. 18:9)

Abraham was married to his sister, Sarah. As he said to Abimelech, "She truly is my sister also, the daughter of my father though not of my mother; and she became my wife." (Gen. 20:12)

Cain was married to his own sister. So was Seth. For them, there was no other choice. That was by God's design. At a certain point in time, after Abraham, God forbade such marriage.

Was it then the law of the Rabbis that Abraham kept? No. There were no rabbis in the time of Abraham, and there wouldn't be any for about 2,000 more years. When the Rabbis did appear, they claimed authority for their laws in the Law of Moses.

Here's a simple example. In the Law of Moses, God commanded Israel, "Do not cook a young goat in its mother's milk." (Ex. 23:19) Rabbinic prohibitions against eating milk and meat together are said to be derived from this commandment.

Rabbi Hertz speculated: "thou shalt not seethe. This command is repeated in XXXIV, 26 and Deut. XIV, 21. Upon these words, the Rabbis based the prohibition against eating meat and milk together in any way or form whatever. This prohibition was doubtless observed long before the age of the Rabbis; and in connecting it with this text, they merely sought a support in the Torah for an immemorial Jewish practice." [1] In other words, the rabbinic prohibition does not come from this verse, it is merely tied on to this verse.

Actually, in tying the rabbinic prohibition to this verse, the Talmud does not prohibit eating milk and meat together, unless the milk is boiled and the meat is in contact with it. As in Nazir 37a: "It is, therefore, the fact that if soaked in milk all day long, [the meat] remains permitted, and yet on seething it becomes forbidden." (Cf. Pes. 44b)

Whatever the source of the comprehensive rabbinic prohibition, which includes the preparation of meat and milk together as well as the eating of them together, Abraham did not keep rabbinic law. When he was showing hospitality to visiting angels, "He then brought some curds and milk and the calf that had been prepared, and set these before them. While they ate, he stood near them under a tree." (Gen. 18:8) To reconcile Abraham's actions with rabbinic law, some claim that the milk and meat were brought separately, hours apart. The text does not support such a claim.

We know that Jacob also did not live according to the Law of Moses, nor according to the law of the Rabbis. Neither had been given yet. The Law of Moses is explicit: "Do not take your wife's sister as a rival wife, to uncover her nakedness, in the other's lifetime." (Lev. 18:18) The Rabbis add that one cannot even betroth one's wife's sister while the wife lives. (Kid. 50b-51a) Yet Jacob did both of these things. He betrothed Rachel after he was married to Leah, and then he married Rachel as a rival to Leah during her lifetime. (Gen. 29)

We can see what commandments, statutes, and laws Abraham kept by observing his relationship to the land God promised him. "The LORD appeared to Abram and said, 'To your offspring I will give this land.'" (Gen. 12:7; cf. 13:15) Abraham did not fight to obtain the land. God did not tell him to do that. God did not tell Abraham to do anything specific to obtain the land. His only responsibility was to believe that God would keep His promise, and live accordingly..

In doing that, Abraham let his nephew Lot choose the best land. (Gen. 13:9) When Lot, the other inhabitants of Sedom and 'Amorrah, and their possessions were taken captive, Abraham could have easily taken over the land. Instead, he fought to rescue them. He then gave to the Lord a tenth of all, in recognition of God's ownership of heaven and earth. (Gen. 14:18-29)

Abraham could have been enriched by all the possessions he had rescued, and in that way become the lord of the land. The king of Sedom encouraged him in that. But Abraham refused, because he was trusting God to provide in His own way, in His own time. (Gen. 14:21-24) He focused on God, not on what he could get.

God responded by affirming their relationship, which was Abraham's true wealth. "After this, the word of the LORD came to Abram in a vision: Do not be afraid, Abram. I am your shield, your very great reward." (Gen. 15:1)

Years later, God told Abraham that He was about to destroy Sedom and Amorrah. Abraham could have thought, "Wonderful. Now I will be able to inherit the land God has promised to me." Instead, Abraham interceded with God to spare the cities and their inhabitants.

In His covenant with Abraham, God — the Creator and Owner of heaven and earth — gave the land of Israel to Abraham and his descendants as an everlasting possession. The calling of Abraham and God's promise to him were given to Isaac, then to Jacob (whom He called Israel), and then to Jacob's descendants. (Gen. 12:7; 13:15; 15:18; 17:8; 26:4; 28:13; Ps. 105:8-11; Gen. 21:12; 25:23) In God's relationship with the Jewish people, the land of Israel is a central part of His promise. It is a central part of Abraham's calling, and it is a central part of the coming kingdom of God.

And yet, Abraham never tried in any way to get the land. It was not because he was unwilling to fight for what God had entrusted to him. It was simply that, "To everything there is a set time, a time for every purpose under the heavens. ... a time of war and a time of peace." (Eccl. 3:1,8) God has His times and His purposes. It was not God's time.

God told Joshua and his generation to fight, take the land, and set it free from the abominations of those living on it.) Joshua and Abraham needed to be able to hear from God in order to know the times and seasons of His purposes. All of Abraham's children need to be able to do the same.

God expected Abraham to be faithful, to trust and obey Him. That is what Abraham did. This was the guiding rule, the law by which Abraham lived. He lived by a law of faith; i.e. trusting and obeying God no matter what. That is what his children must do as well. "The righteous will live by his faith." (Hab.2:4; Rom.1:17; Gal.3:11; Heb.10:38)

In this, the Talmud agrees. It says that God gave to Israel 613 commandments through Moses; David, in Psalm 15, reduced them to 11; Isaiah [33:15-16] reduced them to 6; Micah [6:8] reduced them to 3; Isaiah [56:1] then reduced them to 2; "But it is Habakkuk [2:4] who came and based them all on one, as it is said, 'But the righteous shall live by his faith.'" (Makkot 23b-24a)

The one who lives by his faith in God will fulfill all that God requires of him. As it is written, "Abram believed the LORD, and He credited it to him as righteousness." (Gen. 15:6)

God said of Abraham, His friend, "I have known him, so that he may command his children and his household after him to keep the way of the Lord by doing righteousness and justice; in order that the Lord may bring upon Abraham what He has spoken about him." (Gen.18:19) Abraham's faithfulness meant that God could depend upon him, and could do for him all that He wanted to do. May the same be said of you.

---

1. <u>The Pentateuch and Haftorahs</u>, edited by J.H. Hertz, Soncino Press, London, 1956, P.318

**You will find more information that is helpful at**

**www.elijahnet.org**